The Opening of the Lotus

The Opening of the Lotus
Developing Clarity and Kindness

Lama Sherab Gyaltsen Amipa

Wisdom Publications · London

Published in Holland as *Training van de geest*
by Ankh-Hermes in 1986. Published in Switzerland as
Geistesschulung im tibetischen Buddhismus by
Ansata-Verlag in 1986

Published in England in 1987

Wisdom Publications, 23 Dering Street, London W1, England

© Lama Sherab Gyaltsen Amipa 1987

British Cataloguing in Publication Data
Amipa, Sherab Gyaltsen
 The opening of the lotus: developing clarity and
 kindness
 1. Buddhism–China–Tibet
 I. Title
 294.3'923   BQ7604

ISBN 0 86171 049 5

Set in Garamond 11 on 13 point by Setrite of Hong
Kong and printed and bound by Eurasia Press of
Singapore on 80 gsm cream Sunningdale Opaque
paper supplied by Link Publishing Papers of West
Byfleet, Surrey.

Contents

Foreword

I am very glad to know that venerable Geshe Lama Sherab Gyaltsen Amipa is bringing out a book on the foundation of Dharma practices, *The Opening of the Lotus*.

Firm foundation is very essential for doing Dharma practices and I am sure this book will certainly help many ardent students in practising the sadhanas correctly.

I sincerely wish all success to venerable Geshe Lama Sherab Gyaltsen Amipa and his followers in bringing out this needy book and the many practitioners who will benefit immensely from this book.

HIS HOLINESS SAKYA TRIZIN
Head of the Sakyapa Order
of Tibetan Buddhism
Dehra Dhun,
Uttar Pradesh, India.

Preface

Many people today have developed an interest in connecting the religions of East and West. I find this interest very valuable, and through my relationships with people in the West have gained new insights. All these people seek to follow a path of peace, and from their aspiration to connect Eastern and Western religions they have begun to learn about Buddhist philosophy and meditation. Peace must come from the mind, so in this book I try to explain the various methods for training the mind according to the teachings given by the Buddhas of the past. I also draw upon my own experiences gained from study and from my relationships with people in the West.

I have included here teachings from both the Hinayana and Mahayana paths. The first part of the book mostly gives an explanation of the methods of mind training. The second part contains fundamental Buddhist ideas and the third part explains basic Dharma practice. For deeper Dharma practice it is necessary to obtain teachings from a qualified teacher, a guru. A correct understanding of the Dharma is of the first importance since it enables us to enter meditation.

How are we to practise the Dharma? Firstly we have to listen to the Dharma and try to comprehend its meaning. For the beginner it is essential to understand the significance of terms such as the six paramitas (perfections), the five paths, and the ten levels. We have to master the preliminary practices, and through this understanding we can try to control the mind; then once the mind is controlled, we can start to meditate.

I sincerely hope this book will be of use to those who wish to practise the Dharma. During the seventeen years I have spent in Europe, mainly in Switzerland, I have had the chance of leading a very comfortable life. This fills me with great gratitude and it is from this gratitude that this book originates. I dedicate the merit accumulated by this virtue to universal peace and happiness and the early attainment of enlightenment by all sentient beings.

Lama Sherab Gyaltsen Amipa

Introduction
Buddhism in Tibet

OM SVASTI: HOMAGE TO THE GREAT COMPASSION!
A million sunbeams dance from behind the golden
    mountains,
They pervade and illuminate the world,
Yet more brilliant is the golden body of Buddha;
    radiant with the marks, and signs of perfection.
May his lotus feet always rest upon the crown of
    my head.
Taking birth as a human being in successive rounds
    as the incarnation of the great and mighty Man-
    jusri,
You became famous as Kunga Gyaltsen.
During the twenty-fifth incarnation hailed by all as
    the great master,
To you I make my obeisance.

The teachings of Lord Buddha first began to flourish in
Tibet during the seventh century AD. Although the Buddhadarma first appeared in India, it gradually spread to
many countries to the East and West, and eventually Tibet
became the chief sanctuary for the blessed teachings. This
occured because a number of Tibetan translators travelled to
India and translated a vast number of discourses by the
Buddha and treatises by Indian panditas and siddhas from
Sanskrit and other languages into Tibetan. These translators
did not merely translate from their own personal interpretation. Rather, they followed the Tibetan king's command that

they work with teams of qualified Indian panditas. These translators were, in fact, emanations of Buddhas and bodhisattvas. Their final translations were presented to a number of Tibetan and Indian panditas for them to inspect, and they were not included among the scriptures until they were found to be flawless.

Another reason for the superb quality of these translations is that the written Tibetan language was constructed on the basis of Sanskrit specifically in order to translate the Buddha's discourses and the later Indian Buddhist treatises. Each word and phrase of the original manuscripts was thus translated directly into Tibetan without ambiguity or imprecision. On this solid foundation, the entire body of the Buddha's Hinayana, Mahayana and Vajrayana discourses and the treatises of later Indian Buddhist panditas were translated into Tibetan.

Before the advent of Buddhism, Tibet had been under the influence of the Bon religion. It was in the reign of King Thori Nyentsan that the sacred Buddhadharma first appeared in Tibet. After the reigns of five successive kings, Avalokitesvara himself appeared in the sixth century in the shape of the pious King Songtsen Gampo. At the age of thirteen, Songsten Gampo took over the leadership of Tibet and, in the course of his reign, set up numerous monasteries and temples throughout the country. It was at this time that a translator by the name of Thomi developed the Tibetan script by using the Devanagari alphabet as a model. At the same time Songtsen Gampo propagated the Buddhist moral discipline of the ten virtues.

After five further kings had succeeded to the throne, Trison Detsun, an emanation of Manjushri, was crowned King. He summoned Khanchen Bodhisattva Santaraksita and Padmasambhava to Tibet and the two masters founded the famous and magnificent Samye monastery. The impulse that originated in Samye spread far and wide, persuading other kings (among them the great King Thiral) and ministers to follow the teaching, which they then practised in succession.

Owing to its different spiritual traditions and their sup-porters, Tibet was divided into several competing dynasties and Buddhism eventually declined. But in the eleventh cen-try there was a renaissance of Buddhism in Tibet. At this time several religious traditions emerged, of which the four most important are the Nyingma, Kagyu, Sakya and Gelug. The differences between these various traditions are based on the varying methods they employ in the practice of the doctrine. However, Tibetan Buddhism does not differ from the Buddhism that was orginally taught in India. All four traditions are based on logic and authentic textual reference, and all adhere to the complete teachings of the Hinayana, Mahayana and Tantrayana vehicles. Indeed, the most vital aspect of Tibetan Buddhism is that the teachings of the three vehicles are recognized by all schools.

Part One
Spiritual Training

Introduction

The chief purpose of spiritual training is the transformation of the mind. This can be accomplished by practising virtue. It must be clearly understood, however, that spiritual training is a long and painstaking process and needs a lot of patience and practice. This as we all know, applies to the body, too. An athlete who wants to be successful must undergo intensive training. It is certainly very difficult to change our mentality, but equally it is possible to make great progress and, in doing so, to acquire vast knowledge. This training should chiefly cause us to abandon our selfishness and to initiate the transformation of our mind. It should, furthermore, enable us to help others, in the following way. Many of the texts involved refer to the following five important points:

1. Foundation practices
2. Meditation on bodhicitta
3. Transformation of obstacles to spiritual freedom
4. Signs of spiritual development during the course of training
5. Advice on spiritual practice.

I *Foundation practices*

These include meditations on: (1) The precious human body; (2) Impermance; and (3) Karma and its fruits. In order to achieve successful spiritual development, it is essential to be completely familiar with these practices. If ever we want to be of use to others, we need to be in command of these methods, just like a good teacher needs a thorough training.

The precious human body

We should realize the importance of our precious human body, with which many useful acts can be performed – provided it is properly cared for. A lot of people live their lives with only one object in mind, that is, to obtain a great number of worldly things, thus wasting their valuable energy. This is a very limited type of existence. If body and mind are used wisely and if the Dharma path is followed, then there are no limits to our abilities. We have the chance to rid ourselves of all difficulties, to acquire virtue and to obtain Buddhahood at last.

Since we are capable of following the spiritual path (by virtue of being born as human beings) it is of great importance to find this treasure within ourselves and, further, to put it into practice. The person who has understood this clearly and yet insists on enjoying the pleasures of samsara will most certainly fall into deeper misery.

Impermanence

We must not postpone this spiritual practice for our own death is certain and the time of our death is unknown to us. It could be at any moment. With this in mind, we must not waste any valuable time, but must follow the Dharma path. Contemplation of the moment of our own death is the best cure for indolence. By realizing this, we are already turning towards the Dharma, not only during our short existence in this world but continuously until complete enlightenment is achieved.

Karma

We take the accomplishments of this present life with us into the next life. This may be compared to a tree which grows higher and higher every year until it eventually bears fruit. It must be our solemn endeavour, therefore, to attain rebirth as a human being. If we fall back down to the lower realms it will be very difficult to obtain a human body again.

In order to avoid rebirth in the lower realms, we can already plant the seeds in the human world by practising the spiritual path. We must be alert in our endeavours and escape both deception and delusion − otherwise we cannot practice the Dharma. To escape from delusion, we must carefully watch over the three precious meanings of body, speech and mind.

Let us practise the ten virtues and do no wrong. Bad habits and failings are of a truly sorrowful nature. If we meditate on these themes, we shall gain security and knowledge by intuition.

2 Meditation on bodhicitta

I shall start this chapter with an explanation of relative bodhicitta. Having understood relative bodhicitta it will be easier to penetrate the meaning of absolute bodhicitta.

Relative bodhicitta

Many people are unhappy, have terrible problems, or feel insecure. By developing bodhicitta, these difficulties can be transformed into healing, thus leading to the path of deliverence. Transformation always produces an opposite result: so, for instance, unfavourable circumstances can be changed into the path to enlightenment, but for this to happen bodhicitta must become firmly established in our minds. The doctrine of bodhicitta is neither a philosophical speculation nor an intellectual conclusion, but an absolute necessity for spiritual training.

Normally, we react to problems defensively, that is, either by blaming other people or our present circumstances. This pattern of behaviour is true of individuals, of nations and also of animals. But in fact this reaction is a pretence. The true cause of the problem is the pampered ego, the self. In order to satisfy this self we have often done wrong. We sought the pleasant things of life, loved certain things and despised others. We fought for our possessions and our rights, thus creating even more misery and distress. And all this was to protect and safeguard our beloved self. This form of behaviour can be observed at all levels of existence.

Countless imprints of these wrong deeds have accumulated within us over many lives. The root of all this unhappiness is nothing but our own self. It exercises such power over us that we cannot bear any hardship at all such as hunger or thirst.

There are two ways in which these karmic wrongs can be cleared away. Firstly, by removing the bad seeds by means of the appropriate practice and meditation, which requires supreme effort, and, secondly, by taking upon oneselves the fruits of our own deeds, regardless of what they are. The second is the easier way. By applying this method, to give an example, we should consider it a great help if other people hurt or harm us. By doing so, they provide us with the possibility of freeing ourselves from bad karma. We must recognize that our true enemies are self-love and egotism and that those things which hurt us are in fact actually of great help to us.

If our mind is trained in this way it becomes unchallengeable. In other words, no physical illness can affect us mentally. We all know that if ordinary people fall ill, they also suffer from depressions, which in turn increase their physical discomfort. Bodhisattvas, however, in the same situation, will feel only joy and, hence, will overcome their illness. A well-trained mind is a great asset in our existence where we are constantly confronted with difficulties. The right kind of mental food provides us with strength. For this very reason, problems do not touch bodhisattvas.

We must consider self-love and egotism to be our worst enemies. We should also take all fellow beings as our best friends and render them our assistance. However, we do not as yet have the ability to put this into practice. Therefore, our first goal must be to train our mind accordingly. Let us now be determined to repay the love of all our former mothers and fathers (as embodied in all beings). It should be our aim to help them and to satisfy all their needs. They themselves strive for happiness. By rewarding them with our love, we exercise our mind in the method known as giving and taking. In practice, however, taking comes first. For example, if we want to fill a dish with good food, we must clean it first. Likewise, we should be resolutely prepared to take upon ourselves the sorrows of all beings. We should regard their sufferings as black rays which approach us from the ten directions and which then enter into us. Then we must develop the determination to give happiness, virtue and merit to all living beings. Again, our determination is accompanied by a devout prayer to our object of refuge in order that it may be fulfilled. At this point we visualize rays of light going out to all living beings, bringing them happiness and merit. This exercise should be repeated very frequently.

By practising constantly, Buddhahood will gradually be achieved and this will benefit all beings. The chance of giving direct and effective help to all beings only exists when all the attributes of a Buddha have been acquired. The performance of these exercises is very difficult to begin with since we are not used to caring for other people in this way, nor do we have any experience of this way of thinking. The best way to practise, therefore, is to start with our problems, with the sorrow and misery that we feel at this moment, and with those burdens which are still to come, either in the future or in the next life. The understanding which we have developed and gained by exploring our own suffering can then be extended to all beings, thus giving them the help they need. This must be our aim. Although it may be difficult to begin with, later on it will come spontaneously, and it will also prove a blessing to the one who practises sincerely.

Normally, our reaction to pleasant things is one of attachment, whereas hatred arises when unpleasant things come our way. To neutral things we usually respond with indifference. Let us refrain from attachment and give all beings love and wisdom. Whatever is sorrowful, let us take it upon ourselves, and let all others share the merits of our good attributes. If we practise this in earnest, our own sufferings will be increasingly eased and we shall find ourselves in a position to change our adverse circumstances. This transformation from negative to positive situations will be an aid to enlightenment. We desperately need this help, as a bird needs a rising current of air. Let us take on the difficulties of all beings and in return give them happiness and virtues.

Not only in meditation, but whenever we have the chance, we should put this method into practice, for otherwise we are letting ourselves down. Let us keep this in mind and beware of bad actions. At every moment we should be prepared to give and take while we are eating, sleeping, or during whatever activity we may be engaged in. We are breathing at every moment of the day. Let us perform a useful deed with each and every breath. We should remember that we are looking after our body in order to serve others. This should be our sole task. We listen to the teachings of the Dharma in order to develop the right attitude to help others. If we use all our energies to practice the Dharma our life will be of value. This is the time when we have the chance to practise. Let it be our solemn endeavour.

Absolute bodhicitta

It is through our ignorance that we think all things have an independent self-existence — hence, all living creatures have to suffer in samsara. Suffering is caused either by human beings or by other circumstances.

Ignorance is always present. We can readily recognize it when we observe emotions, such as exasperation, happiness or fear. This is when we experience our self-clinging very strongly. We must observe ourselves closely for months or even years in order to realize the truth of this. Only then are we able to perceive sunyata – the negation of the independent existence of phenomena. In other words, phenomena which we consider to be genuine are in reality like the illusions of a dream. For this very reason, the recognition of sunyata ("emptiness") is most important. It should not only be realized by means of oral or written instruction, but through continuous meditation.

We are in the habit of looking at things as though they existed independently of our own consciousness. This view we know to be wrong, and if we adhere to it, we will be exposed to delusion. Therefore, it can be said that phenomena do not exist in the way we understand them to but neither can their existence be denied, for this would be the opposite extreme. We who have been living with ignorance for so long are not of course in a position to differentiate and we consider our own conception to be the only true one. It is the real meaning of sunyata, however, which represents the only true existence.

Through sunyata it may seem to us that things are non-existent. However, they are not entirely illusions as dreams are. These things or phenomena do have their own existence. For example, if we look at snow through yellow-tinted glasses, the snow appears to be yellow. The glasses distort our perception. Likewise, our ignorance also makes things look distorted and they seem naturally self-existent, like the yellow snow. The way in which these objects exist, however is entirely different from our perception of them. But, as already mentioned, we must not fall into the other extreme by denying these objects their existence.

Let us be sensible and steer a middle course. Let us direct our attention to sunyata, the emptiness or negation attached to all phenomena.

3 Transformation of obstacles into spiritual freedom

The unfavourable circumstances in which people have to live must be changed into deliverance and freedom. Human beings suffer from wars, illness, poverty, mental problems, personal failings, and the like. These unfortunate circumstances are the result of our former impure actions. People without any spiritual training will find it very difficult to practise the Dharma under these adverse conditions. Only those who have developed bodhicitta can be their rescuers.

The problems we meet have their roots deep in our self-loving, egotistical attitudes. This is why we should rejoice when we are forced to harvest the fruit of impure karma for which we ourselves planted the seeds. Why should we be disappointed at something which we ourselves inflicted? As an example, if you find yourself practising the Dharma earnestly and you are deprived of your home or if you have to flee from your own beloved country, you must be aware of the fact that, in former times, you might have performed a deed which led to this misfortune. Therefore, you should pray and develop the strong desire to take on all the sufferings that other beings have to bear. If you have this attitude, you may be deprived of your home, but you will still adhere to Dharma practice. You should react in the same way when you are insulted or ridiculed without having done harm to anyone. Normally, one reacts to this with ill-feeling, but if you wish to practise Dharma you should think of the merits you may gain. Those who harm you are actually helping you to reduce your karmic debts. Therefore, think of them with kindness. In the future, you will be on your guard against performing bad deeds, for you know the outcome. Whatever your negative circumstances may be, use them as an important precondition for meditation.

Wherever you live, even if it is in a cave, and whatever bad things may happen, make good use of them all and develop an understanding of sunyata. No weapon directed at you can inflict injury, because then you are at peace with yourself. Progress and strength are your virtues. Sakya Pandita, one of the Mahasiddhas of Tibet, said: 'While I am sleeping, walking and eating, always I meditate.' By acting in this way, we can do no wrong and we also gain merit. Our thoughts, speech and actions are directed towards the Dharma. Once the spark of bodhicitta is produced, it has the same effect as pouring oil on a fire, and it lays the foundation for further development.

4 *Signs of spiritual development during the course of training*

An ever-joyful mind is already a sign of good progress. Wrong doing can thus be eliminated and we can even regard it as a pleasure when somebody does us harm, for this furthers our progress. However, if we show signs of disappointment and ill humour, as someone who has not practised would react to unpleasant things, then it means that our efforts have been unsuccessful. We can make this observation ourselves, without a guru, simply by testing our reactions.

Self-love and egotism must be transformed into spontaneous charity. We spend most of our time in empty talk and worldly affairs; it would be better to occupy ourselves with the continuous development of bodhicitta.

People who act truthfully and with understanding will recognize the law of karma and its fruits. They protect themselves by controlling their speech and avoid the harmful deeds which can be produced by the three aspects of body, speech and mind.

True ascetics bear all difficulties in order to free themselves of delusions and impure karma. The ordinary person will make sacrifices for the sake of wealth, passion, and the like whereas ascetics make every sacrifice for the Dharma. Those whose deeds conform entirely to the development of bodhicitta are called great sramanas. Those who use all their mental strength to develop bodhicitta and, at the same time, increase their knowledge, are called great yogins and yoginis.

5 *Advice on spiritual practice*

As already mentioned, our daily activity mainly consists of worthless deeds. They should be avoided and efforts should rather be made to help others.

Do not eat out of greed, but for the sake of keeping your body in good health so that you are able to help your fellow beings. Look after yourself in order to reach a ripe old age so that you can practise the Dharma. Likewise, clothes are intended to protect your body against the wet and the cold; they are not meant to be worn for their elegance.

In short, everything is meant to enhance the development of bodhicitta. While developing bodhicitta, we are confronted with a lot of grief caused by all kinds of living beings, but whatever happens, let us remember that our only task is the achievement of enlightenment for their sake and the sake of all beings. If we experience delusions, we must remember that we can use them to banish our indolence, and we must be determined to abandon them. We should get up in the morning with the intention of avoiding all useless deeds and of using our body, speech and mind for the development of bodhicitta. At the end of the day, we should reflect on our actions. If we have done good, we rejoice — if we have done evil, we feel repentance and think of the consequences.

If you lead a comfortable life, you must not forget that all things are impermanent. You cannot rely on your worldly status. If difficulties come about, you should neither be discouraged nor depressed. Difficulties belong to the nature of samsara. You should overcome your troubles and practise bodhicitta.

We should eliminate the ten non-virtues and self-love or egotism. By changing them into just the opposite, bodhicitta is obtained and deep, continuous future sufferings are avoided. Also, three major difficulties must be overcome: (1) the difficulty of recognizing delusions as such; (2) the difficulty of avoiding their renewed appearance once you have recognized them; and (3) the difficulty of interrupting the flow of delusions.

Gather the three main virtues which lead to the end of all suffering: (1) find the guru who shows you the way; (2) be of a virtuous mind so that you can joyfully and with trust practise the Dharma; (3) be wise and active.

Meditate on the three non-diminishing subjects: (1) the non-diminishing reverence for the guru; (2) the non-diminishing joy and happiness of developing bodhicitta (3) the non-diminishing willingness to give help to all beings.

Let us extend our bodhicitta practice to all living beings. All our thoughts must be directed towards bodhicitta. Let us think with compassion of all those who lost their lives in war and who are still suffering at the present time. These disasters which have actually happened and which will always continue, very often form the topic of films, books, plays, and so on. Let us not look upon them as entertainment, however, but with sorrow. Also, when observing powerful political leaders or successful people in business, we should think of the precious human form which we have obtained in this life and which should not be wasted. Let us recognize the real meaning of life.

To give an example of this if we hear the beating of a drum, for example we should remember that an animal had to lose its life for the skin used in the drums. We too will have to leave bodies behind one day. These warnings may well help us in Dharma practice.

Respect your father, your mother and your guru. To despise them is far worse than having similar feelings towards other people. The danger of incompatibility is greater if people live close together. Therefore, you must respect those closest to you — your father, mother and guru. Furthermore, respect your friends and those with whom you have close contact, as well as those who are academically on the same level as you. Exercise vigilance when you are being insulted or when as a result of former karmic connections, you build up aversions.

Exercise detachment from circumstances, whatever they may be. Exercise trust in your practice and consider it to be fertile. Leave difficulties behind you. Everything comes and goes like the wind.

Once you meet your guru and learn about the Dharma and the precious bodhicitta, you must practise intensely. It is up to you. Do not waste your time on senseless worldly matters, but take the opportunity of practising the Dharma.

The six false acts are: (1) Taking pleasure in worldly things instead of practising the Dharma. (2) Having greed for worldly things instead of practising the Dharma. (3) Enjoying worldly things in bad taste, which often goes together with hatred, instead of enjoying the pleasant taste of the Dharma experience. (4) Having compassion for people who are living in poverty but who are practising Dharma, instead of having pity on people who are only seemingly happy. (5) Having false loyalty towards friends and family, which may lead away from Dharma. (6) Having malicious glee at your enemy's misfortune instead of taking pleasure in those who practise the Dharma for the sake of their enemies.

Practise with perseverance. Interruption of the practice hinders progress.

Focus your whole personality firmly on the goal.

Analyse your delusions shrewdly and observe your reactions. Try to eliminate delusions entirely.

Never boast about your great deeds.

Continue the practice until it shows results.

Do not practise the Dharma for praise. Your motivation to help others must be entirely sincere.

All that you do must be entirely unselfish.

A practitioner once wrote:

> My main practice consists of bodhicitta which involves many methods. Regardless of my own sufferings and without considering either praise or reproach, I entirely sacrifice my own self for the sake of those who live in sorrow so that they may experience bodhicitta. Thanks to the instructions of my guru, I could abandon selfishness and for this very reason I can die without regret!

These teachings are easy to understand. They are of supreme importance and indispensable in our degenerate age. We long for happiness and peace, things which do not just come about of themselves. Each one of us has to make our contribution. This represents the method of the great teachers in the past from whom we may learn to act entirely in line with Dharma practice.

Part Two
The Key
to Deeper
Understanding

I *Parting from the four attachments*

This is the written guidance on parting from the four attachments by means of spiritual training:

> To him, whose great wisdom pervades all knowledge like a divine path,
> Whose moonlight-like compassion is the crowning adornment of living beings,
> Whose deeds, like a jewel granting every wish, fulfill all our desires and needs.
> To him, the unrivalled protector, the lion of the Shakyas, the saviour, I bow!
> To Manjushri, who embodies the wisdom of all the conquerors of the three kalpas,
> To Avalokitesvara, who promised to protect all the beings of the three realms.
> To Sakyapa, who took human form to lead all living beings through our depraved days.
> To these three Deities, in all their greatness, respectfully I bow!

Because of the virtues which had been accumulated in former times, we were given a precious human body. With this precious body we were also given the possibility of practising the holy Dharma. By presenting offerings to the guru and the Dharma, spiritual virtues are instantly gained. Those with the pure spirit of virtue will always seek this fulfillment. This text contains exceptional instructions on the significance of Mahayana Buddhism. The pure, perfect

Buddha possesses the mental strength to show all beings the right way.

All instructions on contemplation, vigilance and meditation are disclosed in the Paramitayana and Tantrayana. The proper practice is based on compliance with the written directions as well as on the pursuit of the essential oral instructions.

In the following, some of the most important written directives are given. In Buddha Maitreya's *Abhisamayalamkara* it says that the meaning of the *Prajnaparamita Sutra* is laid down in the graduated path of the *Abhisamayalamkara*.

The *Sutralamkara* teaches the various ways of thinking according to the Mahayana Sutra Collection, that is, the graduated path of contemplation, the devotion for the Dharma, and so on.

Arya Nagarjuna's instructions in the *Madhaymika Ratnamala* are such that higher ways of existence and finally even enlightenment can quite definitely be obtained if the graduated path is followed, the path being based on faith and wisdom.

Acharya Aryadeva teaches the following: parting from the four attachments, and Buddha as the object of meditation — these two things represent the way of life led by those bodhisattvas who have overcome the last obstacles of mental darkness and its cause. Such conduct is the real foundation of the practice. This is the essence of the teaching of the graduated path.

Acharya Santideva says that it is possible to practise the six paramitas with the fully endowed human body. These six paramitas are the essentials of a bodhisattva's existence. If they are practised with devotion the aspirant will be on the graduated path leading to Buddhahood.

Pandit Atisha says that a person with only modest abilities will abandon the greed for this life, thus gaining favourable conditions for the next life. A person with average abilities will abandon the fruits of samsaric well-being whereby deliverance is achieved. A person with highly-developed abilities seeks only Buddhahood, for the sake of all living beings. These three different types of people, with their various abilities, represent the individual steps leading to the path of enlightenment.

The prominent Chandrakirti teaches the following: by practising great compassion as well as bodhicitta, and by acknowledging non-duality, every ordinary person can reach the stage of an arya. By means of the ten paramitas they will then proceed on their way through the ten different stages. This supreme, immaculate tradition of the graduated path for the attainment of the three Buddhakayas (Buddha bodies), was faultlessly disclosed by great philosophers in the Mahayana Tripitaka. However, the written tradition can only be absorbed by a trained mind. A less trained mind will fail to comprehend it.

The second part of the teaching consists of the equally important practice of oral teaching. There are many oral teaching traditions but the most important ones are those handed down by Lama Serlingpa to Atisha and those Manjushri passed on to the great yogi, the Sakya Lama, Sachen Kunga Nyingpo. Lama Serlingpa's oral tradition consists of the following: (1) the difficulty of obtaining a fully-endowed human body; (2) death and impermance; (3) karma, the law of cause and effect; and (4) the adverse conditions of samsara. These four parts of the tradition form the base for generating bodhicitta. You should prepare yourself by meditating on love and compassion which, in turn, is the basis of the main bodhicitta meditation, the chief characteristic of the latter being the exchange of your own self for others. In due course, you should also meditate on absolute bodhicitta.

The path can be defined as follows: (1) unfavourable circumstances lead to the path of enlightenment; (2) your conduct in life is directed towards the Dharma. The studies have various characteristics. They include vows and various methods for training the mind. If they are put into practice, then gradually the unique fulfilment of this great path will occur.

It was Atisha who spread this tradition in Tibet. He handed it down to Geshe Dromtonpa, and to him alone, who passed it on to the three Prominent Brothers and, again, to no one else. These three then spread the teachings throughout the country. In Tibet, this traditional path is as well known as the sun and the moon. With regard to the practice of this path, one may refer to Gyaltse Chözong and his disciples or else to the teachings of Shönnu Gyalchog.

The oral tradition according to Manjushri

This teaching is in accordance with the method of Lama Serlingpa, mentioned above. It does, however, differ from other teaching methods, and it is known to be of a very high standing. Manjushri passed these teachings on to the Sakyapa Lama on the following occasion. When the great Sachen Kunga Nyingpo was twelve years of age, he practised the Manjushri sadhana. After meditating for six months, Manjushri appeared and addressed him in the following words.

> If you have attachment to this life, you are not a
> religious person.
> If you have attachment to the world of existence,
> you do not have renunciation.
> If you have attachment to your own purpose, you
> do not have the enlightenment thought.
> If grasping arises, you do not have the view.

This short and precise explanation includes the practical experience of all the paramitas together. It means that the mind is directed towards the Dharma, if we abandon greed for this life.

If we abandon the greed for samsara, then the Dharma path is followed. If, in ourselves, we wish for nothing, then we clear the path of all delusions. If we abandon the greed for the four extremes, then we cause delusion to be transformed into wisdom.

In preparation, we should meditate on the difficulty of obtaining a fully-endowed human body. The fundamental practice consists of the meditation on death and impermanence. The next theme of the path is the meditation on the law of cause and effect.

Meditation on the difficulty of obtaining a fully-endowed human body

Seated in a comfortable position, take refuge in the guru and in the Three Jewels. Say your prayers to all four so that the mind may turn towards the Dharma. Contemplate the fact that for the sake of all living beings you wish to obtain Buddhahood, thus producing the enlightenment thought. The fully gifted human body features eight freedoms and ten talents which are all difficult to obtain. In order to obtain a fully-endowed body, the virtues of the mind must be developed first. These are rare and difficult to obtain.

Of all the beings in the six realms, only very few are in the higher realms, whereas many, many beings exist in the lower realms. The following example illustrates this relationship. It is said that more insects live in one single hollow tree than there are human beings in the world. This proves that the chances of obtaining a perfect human body are very slight. We must, therefore, be sure not to squander the precious human body which we obtained and to make this a strong subject for meditation. Future lives should benefit by it.

Meditation on death and impermanence

As before, we must take refuge, produce the enlightened thought of bodhicitta and contemplate as follows. Death is certain. Having been born, no living person has ever existed to the end of time. Furthermore, life is uncertain and we do not know when death will come. Our time may soon be up. Only very few circumstances can preserve life. Death is unavoidable. When the moment of death comes, neither

medicine nor religious rituals nor anything else can prevent
it. In the face of death, all material things dwindle. We can
take neither our wealth nor our possessions with us. Only
the Dharma can accompany us on our journey. Bearing this
in mind, we should be able to part from our attachment to
this life. This is the most effective method of turning our
mind towards the Dharma. We enjoy the pleasant things of
life — eat good food, wear smart clothes and are surrounded
by friends and relatives. One of these days, though, we must
leave everything behind and tread the path alone. Worldly
things do not last.

Meditating in this manner will help us to part from our
attachment to worldly activity.

Meditation on karma, the law of cause and effect

Again, we must take refuge and produce the enlightenment
thought of bodhicitta. We should contemplate the fact that
we have obtained a fully-endowed human body, which is
very rare. This precious body is transient. For this reason,
we should abandon all our faults before our death and
develop as many virtues as possible. This is of great importance, for practising bad habits leads to rebirth in lower
realms. For example, killing someone will shorten our own
life and stealing from someone will deprive us of our own
wealth.

If we get used to bad habits, we develop the desire to
practise them over and over again, as a result of which we
get reborn in a lower realm and there is little possibility of
escaping it. On reflecting upon this, our determination to
abandon bad actions should be strong.

Exercising the ten virtues, however, has the opposite
effect: rebirth takes place in a realm of peace. Bearing in
mind that cause and effect correspond, we then arrive at the
following conclusion. If we refrain from killing someone,
our own life will be prolonged. Our good deeds or virtues
will become a habit and rebirth will take place in a pleasant

place. When we recognize this, our wish to practise virtues should be very strong. If we have understood the law of cause and effect knowing what to accept and what to reject, then we must put this knowledge into practice.

Parting from the attachment to samsara

In order to proceed on the Dharma path, we must meditate on the shortcomings of samsara. Again, we take refuge and produce the enlightenment thought of bodhicitta.

Samsara — the cycle of birth and death — is divided into three spheres and six realms. The spheres are known as the spheres of desire, form and formlessness. The six realms are those of human beings, animals, pretas or hungry ghosts, hell beings, gods and anti-gods.

The nature of samsara is suffering. Samsara is also the basis from which suffering spreads and, conversely, to which suffering is drawn or attracted, like a store for the future.

Owing to the power of impure or bad karma, creatures relapse into loathsome situations and experience unbearable suffering in the cycles of existence.

Suffering prevails in samsara. Whichever of the three spheres we are born in, we will always experience the problems of samsaric existence. For this reason, the Dharma path must be fully understood and properly practised so that we can free ourselves from all its various joys and sorrows. We must meditate on the necessity to cut our attachment to samsara and to cultivate the need for deliverance from it.

With regard to the graduated path, the teachings for those with modest and average abilities (refer to page 36, Pandit Atisha) are here concluded. With regard to Lama Serlingpa's explanation concerning the four Dharmas as preparatory exercises, these teachings are also now completed (refer to page 37, Lama Serlingpa's oral teachings).

2 Parting from grasping

By abandoning grasping, the path is cleared of delusions. We must meditate on love, compassion and bodhicitta.

The meditation on love

It is not enough to free our own self from the sufferings of samsara. During countless rebirths in samsara, all sentient beings have at some time been our kind and loving mothers. We must develop the determination to create peace and happiness for all beings. Our mind must be set in such a way that we imagine the kindness our present mother showed us. She looked after us, fed us and gave us clothes, so we should be concerned that she find peace and happiness. The same is true for our father and our other relatives, and for our enemies also, even if they harm us, as well as for all beings in the lower realms. They all suffer terribly and it is up to us to offer help.

The meditation on compassion

As mentioned before, we think of our mother's kindness to us and, at the same time, we wish to free her from suffering. We feel compassion for her and meditate that we want to take the suffering away from her. We also concentrate on all the other sentient beings, as was explained above for all of them have shown great kindness to us. Through our meditation we generate compassion, together with the strong desire to free them all.

When love and compassion are aroused, then bodhicitta is produced. Love and compassion are the roots of all Mahayana Dharmas and it is of the utmost importance to cultivate them.

Bodhicitta meditation

There are three stages to this meditation: (1) relative bodhicitta; (2) meditation on the complete identification of oneself with others; and (3) meditation on the exchange of one's own self for others.

Relative bodhicitta

Although we would like to bring peace to all the kind parents of the three realms, we do not have the necessary ability to do so. Even the deities such as Indra, Brahma, and others, as well as the sublime beings of this universe – the sravakas and the pratyekabuddhas – lack this ability. It is only the perfect, pure Buddha who can achieve this. This is why we should pursue perfect Buddhahood for the sake of all beings. We must meditate on this and wish to rescue all sentient beings from the ocean of samsara.

If our actions are based on this spiritual approach, then all the virtuous deeds we perform will set the foundation for Buddhahood. This is the reason why bodhicitta is so highly rated in Mahayana texts.

The meditation on complete identification of oneself with others

As we wish for peace ourselves, so all other beings also wish for peace. Equally, we seek peace for other beings as we seek peace for ourselves. As we wish to avoid suffering for ourselves, so do other beings attempt to avoid suffering for themselves. As we seek relief from suffering for ourselves, so we should strive to prevent suffering for others.

The meditation on the exchange of our own self for others

To give an example of this meditation: although our mother is kind, she still experiences suffering. This is why we must arouse deep compassion for her. This is how we must meditate: 'May all sufferings and failings of my mother's fall on me so that I can experience them myself. May my peace and all my virtue be given to my mother so that she may attain Buddhahood.'

Now we apply this method in a similar way to our other relatives and to all beings whose troubles we hear and see, to our enemies who do us harm, as well as to the beings who are in hell. We include all living beings in this mediation. By meditating like this, we take upon ourselves all suffering from all living beings and we transfer our own peace and virtue to them. In this way we can satisfy their present desires and, finally, attain Buddhahood.

These are the essentials of Mahayana Buddhism and these are the teachings of all the Buddhas of the three times. With this spiritual attitude, we are following the Buddha's own teachings. This form of meditation is necessary in order to avoid misunderstanding, and although there are various other reasons for it we cannot go into them in detail in this chapter.

As far as the other meditation methods are concerned, that is, relative bodhicitta, bodhicitta on identification and bodhicitta on the exchange of our own self, we should proceed in the same way: taking refuge, producing the enlightenment thought of bodhicitta, and so on. Furthermore, we should practise guru-yoga. After each meditation, prayers should be said in order to dedicate or share the merits we have gained. In addition, we should exercise restraint in all our actions, whether walking, sleeping or sitting.

3   Parting from our attachment to the four limitations

By abandoning these four limitations delusions are transformed into wisdom, that is, the understanding of sunyata, which, according to other oral traditions is achieved by samatha and vipassana (see pages 75–76). Vipassana is the meditation on sunyata.

The tradition discussed here deals with the simultaneous practice of the three following meditations: (1) appearances originate in the mind; (2) mind derives from illusion; and (3) illusion has no nature of its own. As these meditations are performed, an understanding arises that all things are illusive and dream-like. Because of this, we can abandon all our attachments. However, if the guru's instructions are ignored and the meditations are performed according to our own interpretation, then delusions will increase. For written instructions alone are insufficient to convey full understanding, especially since the texts do not always include all the instructions.

For the time being, it is essential to attain all possible roots of virtue, and also to make an effort to undertake good deeds. While doing this, however, we should beware of thinking: 'This is considered to be a virtue and this is why I performed it.' It would be better to think: 'I, personally, have performed this virtue in such and such a way.' No pride must arise but rather, the intention to initiate others into performing virtuous deeds. This is the way to gain the *root* of virtue.

Always remember that all our worldly activities are

45

dream-like and illusive. It is most important to keep this in mind as it will lay the foundations for the right view.

The fourfold path

The fourfold graduated path is described as follows: (1) in order to bring about salvation for future lives, the mind turns towards the Dharma; (2) by parting from samsara, we must follow the path to deliverance: this is the Dharma path; (3) by parting from the Hinayana philosophy, we should adopt the Mahayana philosophy, which means that the path is cleared of delusions; (4) by parting from the attachment to all extremes, we come to understand the meaning of ultimate truth. In this way delusions are transformed into wisdom. These are the essentials of the path and we should practise according to these teachings. In order to give our present physical actions a useful purpose, we should perform prostrations and visit sacred places. In order to give our speech a useful purpose, we should praise all Buddhas and bodhisattvas and read sutras which are full of meaning. In order to give our mental activities a useful purpose, we should meditate on love, compassion and bodhicitta. In order to use our wealth wisely, we should make offerings to the Three Jewels and respect the sangha. If these deeds are performed together with pure prayers, then Buddhahood with all its precious qualities is certain.

The following verses by Sonam Senge are a summary of these teachings:

> It is difficult to obtain a human body which is needed for practising the holy Dharma.
> This body is of transient nature though.
>
> Proper knowledge regarding virtues and non-virtues is essential.
> One must know what to adopt and what to reject.
> This leads to devoted practice and is equivalent to the *first step*.

After recognizing the sufferings of all sentient beings in the ocean of samsara, one tries to reach the shores of nirvana.

This results in renunciation and is equivalent to the *second step*.

All beings as countless as the stars have been our kind mothers and fathers several times over.

By exercising love, compassion and the magnificent bodhicitta, we help these beings to salvation which is equivalent to the *third step*.

Whatever may appear, it is born in our own mind.

Mind — being of illusive nature — is based on an accumulation of circumstances which follow the law of cause and effect.

By realizing a situation which is free of illusive nature, we are capable of entering meditation on the ultimate truth of things which is equivalent to the *fourth step*.

One should make offerings to the Three Jewels at every opportunity.

Step by step one should free oneself from the root of bad conduct.

One should provide the unprotected and the poor with what they need.

All these things must be performed together with the activity of *sharing the merit* which is entirely free of the three manifestations.

If this is achieved, one will certainly be blessed with present and future well-being.

4 *Meditation on the precious human body*

Once we have obtained a fully-endowed human body, we have the chance of realizing the end of suffering. We must therefore recognize the indescribable value of this body through which we can free ourselves. A perfect human body contains the eight freedoms and the ten endowments, which are described as follows:

The eight freedoms

These mean that a person is free from:

1. Attachment to wrong views, like atheism and nihilism or the denial of the law of cause and effect
2. Birth in a non-religious, barbarous country
3. Birth in a country where the holy Buddhadharma is not taught
4. Being insane or having under-developed senses
5. Birth in the hell regions where uninterrupted suffering exists
6. Birth in the preta realm where insatiable hunger and thirst prevent the practice of Dharma
7. Birth as an animal, who is not able to differentiate between right and wrong
8. Birth as a long-lived god who enjoys a great many delights and does not recognize the necessity for the practice of Dharma.

If you possess these eight freedoms, you should recognize

the opportunities they bring and should look upon your body as a wish-granting jewel.

The ten endowments

1. To be born as a human being and, thus, to be able to become free
2. To be born in a country where the Dharma teachings flourish
3. To be born with a healthy body and excellent senses
4. Not having committed any of the five 'great offences'
5. To have faith in and respect for the Dharma
6. To be born in an era when a Buddha is present
7. To have received the teachings of the Buddha
8. To be born while the teachings are still alive
9. To be near a monastic community or any other community which practises the Dharma teachings and leads others onto the path of enlightenment
10. To be guided by a compassionate person, a spiritual friend or teacher who assists and supports the practice.

Therefore, once we have obtained this perfect human body we can also shape our own future and by following the path to higher forms of spiritual existence, we can finally realize full enlightenment.

This is why our present life has immeasurable value. Not only can we obtain rebirth as a human being, but we are also in a position to end suffering and attain Buddhahood. Our body is like a boat which takes us across the oceans of samsara. Since we do not know the time of our death, we must begin our efforts to free ourselves immediately.

As a flower appears out of the ground, so is the attainment of a perfect human body the result of cause and effect. It is only through the Dharma practice that the corresponding conditions are produced.

5 The wheel of existence

The red female demon of death who holds the five parts of the wheel of existence between her fangs represents impermanence. The centre of the wheel contains symbols of the three poisons, that is: the pig represents ignorance; the cock represents greed; and the snake represents hatred. On the circumference of this, one black and one white section can be seen. The white section on the left (looking at it from the front) depicts people on their way to deliverance. The black section on the right depicts people on their way to the hell realms. The five parts of the karmic wheel are as follows. Three-quarters of the top half (A+C) represent the realm of the devas and the remaining quarter (D) shows the human world. The lower half holds the realms of the pretas (hungry ghosts) (E), the animal world (B) and the hell regions (F). Six realms of existence were mentioned earlier but in the original Tibetan text on which the pictorial description is based, the devas (gods) and asuras (demi-gods) are together in one region, hence, there are only five spheres.

Seven days before their death, the devas experience extreme suffering. The signs of coming death are shown by certain symptoms. Their flower decoration, for instance, fades and their body and clothes take on an unpleasant odour. The asuras suffer injury and death through their continous fighting with the devas.

Human beings suffer from birth, sickness and death. The rich become poor, the proud are humbled — they are parted from their loved ones. The rich suffer from the fear that they from their loved ones. The rich suffer from the fear that they may lose their wealth and the less well-to-do suffer because they have to fight for their existence. In fact, at any time, all kinds of trouble may come. People are always chasing after desired objects. If they cannot satisfy their wants then they feel deep disappointment. They waste their time on all kinds of unimportant activity trying to improve their standard of living. But when death approaches and none of these sought-after things have materialized, they experience deep regret.

Animals suffer from maltreatment, slaughter and by being made use of to perform laborious work. Some beings in the ocean live in complete darkness and are eaten by their fellow beings.

The pretas who are born in unpleasant places such as deserts suffer from constant hunger and thirst. Their stomachs are enormous but their mouths are as small as a needle's eye and their throats are as thin as the hair of a horse. If they finally succeed in finding food, it is transformed into fire, blood or excrement and they fight over it.

The hell beings suffer from extreme heat, cold and other afflictions. They languish in hell for long periods of time.

Whichever of these six realms, we are born in, suffering is the nature of them all. Rebirth in the wheel of existence, wherever it may occur, is always based on causality and the karmic influences that go with it.

An explanation follows of the twelve elements that are the cause of all existing shape or form. They are all dependent on each other.

1. *Ignorance*
Ignorance is the cause of rebirth in the samsaric spheres. The old, blind woman referred to in the original Tibetan text is shown as an old blind man in the wheel of existence.

2. *Formation*
Just as potters use clay, water and wheel to form pots, so various elements such as father and mother, male and female are needed to produce life.

3. *Consciousness based on causality*
Just as a monkey swings through the jungle, by grasping one branch after another, so our consciousness orientates itself by clinging to one imaginary experience after another.

4. *Name and Form*
As a person is carried across water in a boat, so the consciousness is carried by the body.

5. *The six senses*
The empty house with six windows symbolizes the six thresholds of perception.

6. *Contact*
Here, too, the pictorial description differs from the original Tibetan text. The latter relates to sexual intercourse between two human beings as symbolizing physical contact. The illustration in the wheel of existence merely shows two people shaking hands.

7. *Sensation*
The sensation aroused by physical contact, be it pleasant, unpleasant or indifferent, is illustrated by the image of an arrow which enters the eye of a human being.

8. *Craving*
In the same way as alcholics try to satisfy their craving so people strive for pleasant and inspiring experiences.

9. *Clinging*
This is illustrated by people picking fruit, which symbolizes the desire to obtain the pleasant things in life.

10. *Becoming*
According to the original text, existence is symbolized by a pregnant woman. The illustration, however, shows a couple having intercourse.

11. *Birth*
The illustration shows a woman giving birth.

12. *Old age and death*
Death is shown as a corpse being carried away.

In the top right-hand corner we see Buddha Shakyamuni standing on a bank of cloud, his left hand in the mudra of protection, his right pointing towards the full moon in the top left-hand corner. The mudra of protection symbolizes the protection and shelter which Buddha Shakyamuni grants to those who are reborn in one of the six realms. The full moon symbolizes cleanliness and purity and, at the same time, embodies the third of the four noble truths, that is, the truth of the ending and prevention of all suffering, as was explained by Buddha Shakyamuni in his sermon on the four noble truths.

The four noble truths

The five parts of the wheel of existence symbolize the first noble truth, which is the *truth of suffering*.

The three animals in the centre of the wheel stand for the second noble truth, which is *the truth of the cause of all suffering*.

The black and white sections around the centre represent the karmic influences and connections based on all deeds performed. Through the power of ignorance, which is the first link in the chain of the twelve dependent elements, we are reborn in samsara. All this the demon holds firmly in her mouth and claws. Until suffering and the cause of it are eliminated, there is no escape from this demon of death.

The full moon represents *purification*, which is the third noble truth.

The fourth noble truth, that is, *the true path leading to deliverance*, is embodied by Buddha Shakyamuni.

The Tibetan text on the full moon reads as follows:

> The upright Buddha shows the way. If someone is very attentive, he can control his ego by applying the Dharma method. He can leave Samsara behind and, finally, bring all suffering to an end.
>
> Cease to do evil,
> Learn to practise virtue,
> Purify the mind.
> That is the teaching of all the Buddhas.

6 *Karma*

Because of our bad deeds and our faults, we are born into the sorrowful world of samsara. Before we can free ourselves we have to remove the causes of this servitude. It is only then, that is, after eliminating bad conduct, that we can try, with all our power, to lead a virtuous life. Greed, hatred and delusion — these three are the roots of the ten non-virtuous deeds.

The ten non-virtuous deeds

1. Killing
2. Stealing
3. Sexual misconduct
4. Untruthful speech
5. Harsh speech
6. Slander
7. Frivolous talk
8. Covetousness
9. Malevolence
10. Attachment to misconceptions

If one or more of these non-virtuous deeds is performed, it will inevitably result in painful experience. Such conduct is damaging not only to this life, but to the next as well.

To give an example: if someone kills someone, then this action will shorten their life. And it may result in rebirth in one of the hell realms too. On the other hand, virtuous deeds result in good karma. If the conduct of body, speech and mind is free from the three poisons, then it can only be advantageous. To state the earlier example in reverse: by refraining from killing, one's own life may be prolonged.

By eliminating bad conduct and adopting virtuous behaviour, full enlightenment or Buddhahood will finally be attained. The neutral acts which we perform will also be transformed into virtues. For instance when we eat, we should think of bodhicitta and that we only feed ourselves to keep our body in good health so that we may help others.

Enlightment only develops as a result of certain causes and is not produced by delusion or misunderstanding. Rice which is planted in winter will not grow, for the conditions are not right. In order to harvest a rich crop, well-irrigated fields in a warm climate are necessary. In other words, all the conditions must be favourable.

Likewise, loving kindness and deep compassion for all living beings can only grow on fertile ground and they are the ultimate factors at all stages of the graduated path. They are the only source of bodhicitta, of the bodhisattva stage as well as of the Buddha wisdom. Where love and compassion exist, the seed of bodhicitta can flourish.

7 Love

What then is the essence of love? Love is identical with the strong desire that all living beings find happiness. We think of our own mother's kindness and the fact that all living beings like her in the course of numerous rebirths in the samsaric spheres have been our kind mothers.

Our mother has been exceedingly kind to us. For nine months she carried us and did not complain of the pain and risk of giving birth. She looked after us in our childhood and when we were helpless. She looked at us with loving eyes, cradled us in her arms and sang sweetly to us. She gave us food and clothing. She protected us from danger and showed us the ways of the world. She sacrificed her own needs in order to look after us properly. She always tried her best to smooth our path. She always had our well-being at heart and had it been up to her, she would have made us the conqueror of the universe.

Our mother is not only our mother in this present life: she has been our mother in numerous former lives. Many times she had to beg to fulfill our needs. She committed many offences purely for our sake, saved our life when we were attacked, and even died for us. In previous lives she may have been our father, who also did us one good turn after another. She may have been a relative, a lover or a friend. Even if we gave her the whole world made of gold, we could not repay her kindness.

It is, after all, hard in this round of existence even to be aware of the Three Jewels, Buddha, Dharma and Sangha.

Even the fact that we have the opportunity of practising religion is solely due to our dear mother, and we benefit by it in this life and in the bardo (the transient state between life and rebirth) as well as in the next life.

Now the time has come for us to repay this kindness. What could be better for our mother than happiness. But since we do not have ability to make her happy, we must pray for her and meditate, thus developing a very natural kind of love for her. After this we should extend our meditation to our relatives, our neighbours, our friends and enemies. Then we think of our father and meditate in the same manner until we feel the same devotion for him as we already feel for our mother. After that we extend our meditation to all living beings.

Love for our enemies

The most difficult exercise is to develop love for our enemies. We should therefore proceed as follows: we remind ourselves of our enemy and think that in numerous former lives he or she may have been our kind father or mother. We never repaid that kindness, however, and for this reason this person now appears as our enemy, reminding us of our debt. Since we are all living in ignorance, we are not capable of recognizing this. So we confront one another as enemies. In reality, though, we are very close to each other, as a mother is close to her child, because on numerous occasions we have helped each other in the past. But even under these present unpleasant circumstances, facing each other as enemies, we are still helping each other a great deal. The mere recognition of this motivates us to practise religion and to free ourselves from delusion.

In this way we should try to repay the kindness of our supposed enemy as we would that of our present mother, and although this may be very difficult to start with, we should be aware of the sorrowful consequences which hatred and animosity can bring.

There are none more ignorant than those who claim to practise the Mahayana path and yet hate their enemies. Hatred does not harm the victim but the one who hates. If we do not succeed in fighting our inner enemy, then our worldly enemies will continue to exist in great numbers. However, if we conquer our inner enemy successfully, we shall live untroubled and in peace.

We should think in this way. When we consider our enemies as our former kind parents, then we have developed the right view. All living beings were our parents at one time. This is why we must apply our meditation to all beings. Our daily tasks should consist of rescuing animals and providing the poor with their wants and needs. We should always make an effort to control our speech and be pleasant and kind.

The basis of Mahayana is *love*. With love it is easy to develop compassion. For this reason, the meditation on *love* is of utmost importance.

8   Compassion

Chenrezig (the Buddha of compassion) said in one of the sutras: 'He, who wishes to attain Buddhahood, need not follow various different practices; he must only practise one thing and that is deep compassion!' Wherever compassionate bodhisattvas go, all the Buddhadharmas are present with them.

The objects of this heartfelt compassion are all living beings, and the hope that all living beings may be relieved of suffering is born out of a deeply-felt wish. While meditating on this, we should think of our own mother who has extended her loving kindness to us throughout many former lives and who has experienced great suffering for our sake. She readily accepted those sufferings, for which she should be rewarded by us. It would be best for her if she could be freed both from *suffering* and from the *causes of suffering*, for, at present, she is entangled in a network of sorrow and grief and is even planting the seeds of her own further grief. This is why we must feel deep compassion for her. 'May she be rescued from all sufferings.' This must be our heartfelt wish.

We must pray to the guru and to the Three Jewels, for we ourselves do not have the ability to help. It is the Buddhas and bodhisattvas who have the power and the strength to answer our prayers. We must continue this meditation practice until our compassion reaches all living beings.

The basis of all suffering is ignorance. In order to be free from suffering, it is necessary to remove the causes of suffering. Therefore, all living beings should be relieved of suffering and of its cause — ignorance.

We should practise this meditation over a long period of time, especially with regard to our enemies. For instance, if we extend this meditation to all living beings, then we shall be able to visualize and understand the sufferings of the hell beings, the pretas and others and, at the same time, realize that these sufferings are a result of bad karma, which originates with ignorance.

9   *Bodhicitta*

Is it possible to obtain enlightenment by avoiding bad deeds and by meditating on love and compassion? The answer is that these practices are certainly a great help on our path to enlightenment, but that they are not sufficient by themselves. As long as the obstructing self, the ego, is not eliminated, misfortune keeps sprouting like a weed. Only by removing the root of the ego can suffering be ended. The sufferings of samsara originate in karma – karma is based on impurity and impurity is caused by the ego.

A practical example will show how the ego causes impurity. It is possible that we may mistake a rope for a snake, without any doubt in our mind. In the same way, through ignorance, we may be misled into believing that we possess an ego or a permanent self, whereas, in reality, such a thing does not exist.

As long as we adopt an ego we differentiate between the self and others. This is when attachment to the self and aversion towards others is developed.

The three impurities

This is also how we develop ignorance with regard to the true nature of all things. If we are dominated by the following three impurities, then all our actions are poisoned and we shall rotate endlessly in the cycle or wheel of existence. The three impurities are: (1) self-love; (2) aversion towards others; and (3) ignorance with regard to the true nature of all things.

In this way, all evil is caused by the ego. If we wish to withdraw from samsara, then we must consider our own ego as our own only true enemy. In order to eliminate it, we must practise the two kinds of bodhicitta, that is, relative and absolute bodhicitta, as mentioned earlier. The relative bodhicitta suppresses the ego, the absolute bodhicitta removes the roots of the ego. Therefore, this practice is very beneficial.

In the sutras it says that the universe would be too small to accommodate the merit that bodhicitta practice produces, if this merit had shape or form. By being inspired with bodhicitta our whole nature changes. All actions and deeds undergo great change and we become a child of the Buddha.

Bodhicitta has the following five characteristics: (1) It is like the philosopher's stone which changes ferric matter into gold; (2) it is like a wish-granting gem, which gives its blessing to its finder; (3) it is like the jambu tree, laden with delicious fruit; (4) it is like a brave warrior, destroying all sins; (5) it is like the great fire at the end of the world, destroying all impurities. Hence, bodhicitta is the most beneficial Dharma practice. It is in the nature of bodhicitta that it surpasses samsara as well as nirvana. Bodhicitta expresses the desire to obtain enlightenment for the sake of other beings and to free them from their sufferings. These thoughts produce invaluable merits.

Compassion is the cause of bodhicitta and love is the cause of compassion. For this reason, we must develop the right kind of love which then results in the desire that all beings may be parted from sorrow and may experience happiness.

At present, we do not have the ability to realize our wishes. Only the Buddhas have this power; they can answer all prayers. This is why we must attain Buddhahood in order to lead all beings onto the paths of either the sravakas, pratyekabuddhas, or, the fully enlightened ones, according to the various abilities of the beings.

Meditation on bodhicitta

We should reflect that our parents and all living beings seek happiness. But since they do not know the way to achieve this, they are exposed to extreme suffering, thus producing the causes for even greater suffering. They suffer from delusion and ignorance and they do not have the chance of finding a guru to guide them. They stray away from the path leading to higher realms and enlightenment, and instead they wander onto the steep path leading to the lower realms. We should not only feel great compassion for those beings, but we should endeavour to end their sufferings.

We must be aware of the fact that we are not capable of realizing this ourselves and that only the Buddhas have this power. One single ray of light coming from a Buddha's body can free countless beings. With one sermon alone, a Buddha can relieve all beings from hardship. This is why we must try to reach Buddhahood.

We must send intensive prayers to the guru and the Three Jewels so that they may fulfil our striving for Buddhahood. Even outside meditation practice, we should always wish for enlightenment and Buddhahood.

If we want to reach enlightenment through compassion, then we should try to do as little as possible for ourselves, but do as much as possible for others. It is through selfishness that we are still revolving in samsara to this day.

There never existed such a thing as self; it is we who have created it. We keep cradling and protecting this fictitious self by non-virtuous deeds. This, again, causes suffering. For this reason, we should treat our ego as an enemy and only feel concern for others.

It will not be possible to induce this inner transformation immediately. The first step will be to achieve serenity through continuous meditation, which will then slowly bring about the change. We must also bear in mind that other living beings are striving for the same thing in order to find happiness, and we must be prepared to help them so that they may free themselves from this great burden.

Here the question arises as to whether people should be helped by others rather than helping themselves. How can someone else, as an outsider, remove all the obstacles and clear the path? This can best be explained by a practical example: suppose you have a splinter in your foot, obviously you will try to remove it with your hand and not your foot, although the hand is different from the foot. Of course, it could be argued that both the foot and hand are part of the body, but although both the foot and hand belong to our body which represents a unity, we call them *our* foot and hand and not *we* foot and hand. In other words, although these parts belong to the body, we, nevertheless, accept them as individual members of the body, performing different functions. This, of course, does not mean that we consider ourselves as consisting of various different body members. We look upon ourselves as one coherent creation or, in other words, as a whole. In the same way, we should interpret our relationship to others. When we talk of others we would say *our* fellow beings just as we would say *our* foot.

Our own inner feelings and the feelings of others are one and the same thing. We are all striving for the same things. With this consideration in mind, we should treat our fellow beings as we would treat ourselves.

Assuming what has just been said is correct, we can still make the objection that we are not in a position to help our fellow beings anyway. This is the wrong attitude, however, because determination will help us to make progress in saving others.

In our meditation we should contemplate the fact that beings are as countless as the universe is endless. For the sake of all these beings we must reach Buddhahood by following the meaningful path leading to deliverance. Enlightenment does not take place until attachment to the ego is removed. This is why we must part from our ego because attachment is the root of the problem. We should act with consideration for others and follow the bodhisattva path. We must practise in this way in order to develop true charity.

If we wish to obtain enlightenment without delay, we should reverse our attitude; in other words, we should think of others in the way we are used to think of ourself. However, to obtain Buddhahood, it is not enough to like others in the way we like ourselves. More than this, we must prefer others to ourselves.

All living beings have been our kind mothers through numerous lives and it is only with their help that we can attain enlightenment. For this reason, we should take upon ourselves the suffering and the cause of suffering of all beings. We must develop the desire to offer our happiness and the cause of it to all other beings. We must part from our attachment to ourselves, otherwise enlightenment is not possible.

If we only think in terms of ourselves, then we shall find ourselves fighting for things like food, clothing and privilege; even a few careless words can cause misunderstanding and quarrels. It is not unusual, as we all know, that even between friends and relatives disharmony is caused by these entirely unnecessary events.

Selfishness causes unhappiness and is the root of all evil. We must fight it like our worst enemy. Let us look upon all living beings as our relatives and let us bring them happiness.

If we tried to take on the sufferings of others, we would probably be doubtful and even afraid that we might not be able to take this burden. However, we can be assured that these sufferings do not actually descend upon us. The mere thought of relieving others and taking on their burden is in itself beneficial and does actually alleviate the grief. If we make it a habit to put ourselves entirely at the disposal of others, then we should also be able one day to sacrifice ourselves for others without any hesitation. All great bodhisattvas have acted in this way.

This kind of practice results in Buddhahood. By satisfying the needs of others, our own needs will be met. Had we practised in this way before, we would have reached enlightenment already. Furthermore, we would be in a state of total bliss, far removed from any suffering. But even at this late stage, we should meditate on these subjects intensely.

To start with, we should imagine our own mother who was always kind and deserves our help. She is exposed to suffering and its causes and we want to relieve her of them. All our virtues should be transferred to our mother. Since we have always failed to treat our mother in this way, we have not attained enlightenment.

From now on, for the rest of our lives, we must make the effort to free ourselves from our ego. All actions performed to satisfy our ego must be eliminated. It is through religious practices that we can make amends to our kind mother.

We should firstly visualize our mother in front of us. All the suffering that comes from our mother's heart is absorbed to our own heart. Like the rays of light emmitted by a beautiful sunrise, happiness and its cause flow from our heart to our mother's heart. She will benefit at once by the happiness evoked, and the cause of this happiness will bear fruit at a later date.

This practice is called *tong-len* which means giving and taking: we take on suffering and give away happiness. We extend this practice to our father, friends, and enemies alike, and all living beings, as explained before.

If we suffer great physical and psychological pain, we must remember that innumerable beings suffer equal hardships. None of these beings has asked for these sufferings and therefore we must wish that all the grief of the six realms may come upon us. Let us also bear in mind that suffering is there to try us and that we gain by it. Without hardship, we would have the wrong attitude; we would be lazy and indolent. We would not care about the Dharma and therefore could not turn away from samsara. By suffering now, we can expiate many bad actions which would otherwise descend upon us in a later life.

If we meet with obstacles, evil spirits or enemies, we should apply this *tong-len* method. By doing so, all our present sufferings will be transformed to establish the precondition for enlightenment.

May the sufferings of the three realms descend upon us and may our merits be shared by all living beings. May those who seek the truth find the sublime path through the blessing of this virtue.

10 *Samatha and vipassana*

Samatha

1. The six bends in the road represent the six mental powers. The first stage of mental development – initial fixation, the stage at which you place your mind on the object of meditation, is attained through the mental power of hearing the instructions concerning the meditation from your guru.

2. The stage of initial fixation.

3. The rope represents the mental power of remembrance.

4. The taming hook represents the mental power of alertness.

5. A flame of progressively decreasing size is found from here through the seventh stage of mental development after which it is no longer present. The decreasing size of the flame represents the decreasing amount of effort required in the application of the mental powers of memory and alertness.

6. The elephant represents the mind, and its black colour represents mental dullness.

7. The monkey represents distractions, and its black colour represents mental agitation.

8. The second stage of mental development – increasing fixation – the stage at which you increase your attention span on the object of meditation, is attained through the mental power of thinking about the instructions concerning the meditation.

9. The stage of increasing fixation.

10. The five types of sensory objects represent the objects inciting mental agitation.

11. From here on the black colour of the animals changes to white, starting from the head down. This represents the increasing clarity of the object of meditation and the increasing adherence of the mind to it.

12. The third stage of mental development — patch-like fixation — the stage at which you have the ability to bring your attention back to the object of meditation from an interruption due to mental dullness or mental agitation; and the fourth stage of mental development — close fixation — the stage at which your attention may be brought back even more quickly, are both attained through the mental power of memory.

13. The stage of patch-like fixation.

14. The hare represents fine mental dullness. From this stage you can recognize the distinction between fine and coarse mental dullness.

15. The backwards glance of the animals represents the ability of the mind to return to the object of meditation after recognizing mental wandering.

16. The stage of close fixation.

17. The fifth stage of mental development — invigoration — the stage at which you have the ability to refresh your mind from any fine mental dullness resulting from over-straining to concentrate; and the sixth stage of mental development — pacification — the stage at which you have the ability to sober your mind from any fine mental agitation resulting from becoming too excited when refreshing your mind of fine mental dullness, are both attained through the mental power of alertness.

18. The ability of mental agitation to lead the mind on is curbed.

19. Because thoughts of virtue during the time of the actual samatha cause distraction and interruption to concentration, all such thoughts at that time must be suppressed.

However, at times other than the meditation session, virtuous thoughts should not be suppressed, and the monkey gathering fruit from the tree to the side of the path of meditation represents this distinction.

20.   The mental power of alertness prevents the mind from heeding distractions, and because of the elation which results from this, the mind can be led to samadhi − single-minded concentration.

21.   The stage of invigoration.

22.   The stage of pacification.

23.   The seventh stage of mental development − complete pacification − produces the strength to eliminate the finest mental dullness and agitation. The eighth stage − fixation on a single goal − produces the strength to concentrate uninterruptedly throughout the entire session.

24.   The stage of complete pacification. At this stage it is very difficult for either fine mental dullness or fine mental agitation to arise; and should they arise to even the slightest degree, they can easily be removed with just a small amount of effort.

25.   Here the elephant has become completely white and the monkey is no longer present. With the application of very slight memory and alertness at the start of your meditation, you can enter an uninterrupted state of single-minded concentration in which neither mental dullness, mental agitation nor distractions have the power to cause interruptions.

26.   The stage of single-pointedness.

27.   The ninth stage of mental development − formal fixation − the stage at which you have the ability to retain your attention on the object of meditation uninterruptedly throughout the entire meditation session without having to exert any effort in doing so − is attained through the mental power of complete familiarity.

28.   The stage of formal fixation.

29.   Physical bliss.

30.   The attainment of samatha − mental quiescence.

31.   Mental ecstasy.

32. The root of samsara is cut by a combined meditation on samatha and vipassana with sunyata as the object of meditation.

33. With extremely powerful memory and alertness, represented by the flames, you examine the correct view of voidness.

Vipassana

This is the practice of all-pervading wisdom. If a person seeks mental tranquility and practises samatha, as described above, the mind will be fixed on a single goal and great joy and pleasure will come from it. This is the way in which the bodhisattvas experience it. The nature of this joy is bodhicitta. Vipassana is the basis from which true wisdom arises and it is the essence of all the teachings of the Buddha.

In Santideva's *Bodhisattvacaryavatara* is written:

> This part of the doctrine was taught by the Buddha for the purpose of attaining wisdom. All suffering is eliminated and, by wishing for peace, wisdom is created.

Without the all-pervading wisdom, the clinging to the self or ego, which is the cause of all suffering, cannot be eliminated. Not even Dharma practice, the meditation on emptiness or the performance of the six paramitas can be of any help, if wisdom fails to develop.

The following comparison is given in the *Prajnaparamita*:

> How can a million people on their way find their destination without a guide if they are blind and do not know the way? He who does not have any wisdom is like those people without their eyesight, and without proper guidance he cannot acquire enlightenment.

In the *Abhidharmakosa* it says:

> If one does not possess the differentiating wisdom of the Dharma, then there is no way of eliminating

suffering. Without this wisdom one remains unprotected in the ocean of worldly existence. This is
why the Buddha conveyed the Dharma teaching.

Acharya Saraha said:

He who meditates on sunyata but turns away from
great compassion, will not find the holy path. But
can the one who meditates on great compassion
alone free himself from samsara?
The answer is 'No.'
Just as it is not sufficient to mediate on sunyata
alone without meditating on the non-dual self, so a
mind without any wisdom would not be capable of
removing the root of all wrong conceptions which
show themselves in attachment to the ego.
Therefore, this is not the way out of samsara.

In the *Bodhisattvacaryavatara*, we read as follows:

If the mind does not absorb sunyata, then it leads to
obstacles. It is as though a person were not conscious
of the fact that all things are fundamentally equal.
Therefore, it is important to meditate on sunyata.

In the *Siksasamuccaya*, it says:

The great virtues are created by sunyata and great
compassion. If one strives to become a good, learned
and wise person, then one must exercise compassion.
Moreover, one must realize the phenomenon of the
'non-self.' Only this way can the root of suffering be
destroyed. If one has experienced evenness of temper
as well as complete mental clarity, then very distinct
remembrance is created. These yoga practices are a
part of the ordinary, graduated meditation method.

In order to realize sunyata, one must acquire as many
virtues as possible. Otherwise it is difficult to experience
sunyata. It must be clearly understood that the knowledge
of sunyata alone is not enough. Without virtue one cannot
advance and one will remain on the level of the sravakas.

That is why the *Prajnaparamita* says:

> As long as the basis of all virtues is not fully fertile
> and developed, the meaning of sunyata cannot be
> perceived.

Sakya Pandita says:

> The sravakas also meditate on sunyata but the fruit
> of sunyata is withheld from them. For this reason, it
> is said that the simultaneous practice of method and
> wisdom is the essence of the Mahayana path.

How then can *method* and *wisdom* be practised at the
same time? We should choose a quiet, secluded place and
take refuge in the guru and in the Three Jewels. From the
depths of our hearts we should offer prayers and meditate
deeply on great compassion until bodhicitta is created.

By concentrating on the object of the samatha practice,
we let our mind rest on it for a short while and contemplate
as follows. The peculiar phenomenon of our spiritual nature
is that, from the very beginning, there has been complete
clarity. However, we are deprived of this clarity through
limited mental activity. The distinctness of sunyata means
deep contemplation without any attachment or use of our
imagination. It is through our ignorance with regard to the
dissolution of all combinations that we grasp our self and
cling to our ego, thus getting caught in the never-ending
transmigrations of samsara. The attachment to the ego is a
grave deception which becomes a habit and prevents us from
seeing the truth.

It is of great importance, therefore, to follow the instructions of our spiritual teacher who conveys to us the teachings
of all the Buddhas of the three eras. These teachings have the
deep-rooted power of penetrating the mystery of the mind.

The simultaneous meditation on samatha and vipassana

During the course of the samatha practice, no interrupting
thoughts are possible. During the course of the vipassana

We should always be fully aware of the fact that the following three things have no true nature of their own: (1) the yoga of the meditation; (2) the meditation method; and (3) the person meditating.

The clear uninterrupted mind rests on one point. Hence, we fix our mind on the phenomenon that samatha and vipassana are of the same nature.

During this meditation practice we should think of all living beings, for the final goal is to obtain enlightenment for all.

> May the jewel-adorned boat of divine wisdom reach the remote shores of enlightenment by crossing the ocean of the two accumulations of energy, so that other beings may be helped!
>
> May the glory of the all-knowing Buddha spread the light of eternal joy.
>
> May all my wishes and those of other beings be granted!

11 *The six perfections*

A bodhisattva who wishes to become a Buddha must practise six perfections:

1. The perfection of giving (*dana-paramita*)
2. The perfection of morality (*sila-paramita*)
3. The perfection of patience (*ksanti-paramita*)
4. The perfection of diligence (*virya-paramita*)
5. The perfection of meditation (*dhyana-paramita*)
6. The perfection of wisdom (*prajna-paramita*)

1. *The perfection of giving*

This is divided into four kinds of giving: (1) property; (2) Dharma; (3) refuge; and (4) active love.

Property. The easiest things to give are simple material needs, like food, for example. The most difficult are such things as life, our eyes, and our own flesh, which high bodhisattvas are able to give. The thing we are giving is not the giving – it is only the means for giving. The real giving is the determination to give freely without avarice. So even if we have nothing, we can practice giving, because it depends on the mind, not on the thing given.

At the beginning, giving even money or property is difficult – but after attaining this perfection giving anything, even our own flesh, is easy. To practise it we need a very strong desire to help others, and a very strong will. If we give in order to gain fame, for instance, this is not the practice of giving at all.

Dharma. This is giving the true teaching to other beings, with a pure mind, and it is more beneficial than giving property, which helps only for a limited time. Giving Dharma is lasting, and more deeply helpful. Even people who have sufficient of everything may still suffer. Giving Dharma can remove this and give them a new wisdom-eye. The bodhisattvas striving to attain Buddhahood are also striving to be able to give Dharma as fully as possible to all beings.

Refuge. This means saving the lives of beings, or protecting them from danger.

Active love. The giving of love is the wish to give real happiness to all beings.

All these kinds of giving help in two ways: they help other beings and they help us. If we practise giving for our own benefit, it is not true giving.

2.   *The perfection of morality*

This has three aspects: (1) to protect body, speech and mind from non-virtuous deeds. The tendency towards non-virtuous deeds has to be restrained. This is to stop us from using our body, speech and mind in harmful ways. (2) To protect others in the same way. For instance, if someone is about to kill an animal, we show that it is wrong to do so. (3) To practise virtuous deeds, which automatically protects against non-virtuous ones.

3.   *The perfection of patience*

There are three kinds of patience: (1) patience when someone harms us; (2) patience of suffering and (3) patience of concentration on meditation.

Patience when someone gives us harm. We should not get angry, or react by harming them – we should have no concern for ourselves if we are harmed physically or mentally by others.

Patience of suffering. When we suffer we always point to someone or something outside ourselves as the cause. The immediate reason may be something of this nature, but the deep cause is our own karma, which is our own doing. The results of our own actions always come back to us. We can remember that the seed of suffering has been sown — therefore it must grow. To think like this reduces the power of karma over us. We have to start practising patience with very small sufferings — later we will be able to be patient with very large ones. A bodhisattva can take any suffering for the sake of other beings as a result of having practised the perfection of patience.

To harm someone who is harming us does not make sense from a religious point of view. It does not relieve the pain, but merely creates new suffering for us through karma. If we injure another person with harsh words, the immediate cause of the pain is the words themselves. The words were used by the person who uttered them, but they were produced by the person's delusions. Our anger should therefore, be directed against the defilement. Anger against our fellow beings is very stupid and creates suffering for us. If a country which is being attacked by another country fights back, returning the aggression, it is like a hungry person taking poison. If all people were to practise patience, it would bring real peace into the world. When someone who is struck returns the blow, a chain reaction is set up which has no end. But if one shows patience, the other will do so too as a result.

If we have to walk along a very rocky path, it is impossible to remove all the stones from the way. But wearing strong shoes will protect us from them all.

Patience of concentration on meditation. The third kind of patience is to concentrate patiently on meditation, or anything concerned with Dharma, without allowing distracting influences to harm the practice.

4. *The perfection of diligence*

This means diligence in the Dharma.

The first aspect of this diligence is the mind, which prevents the desire for unprofitable things. If we have a strong desire for ordinary things unconnected with Dharma, it disrupts our Dharma practice. Although we have to do everyday tasks, if our fondness for them is greater than our fondness for Dharma, our attention will be taken away from our main work. If we concentrate and work hard for worldly ends, according to Dharma we are simply lazy. People who really want to practise Dharma are in a hurry not to waste time.

The second kind of diligence protects against tiredness. One way of preventing it is to consider the fruit of meditation and Dharma-practice; if we bear this in mind, physical tiredness will not cause us to lose our energy.

The third kind of diligence is the confidence that we are not too weak to obtain the fruit of Dharma practice. Weakness of this kind stands in the way of achieving fulfilment. It can be overcome by remembering that the highest Buddhas and bodhisattvas also once had only delusion, lived in samsara and were as we are now. By practising Dharma, they reached the highest stage; we can do the same.

The three types of diligence overcome three weaknesses; the first, that the mind will not turn to Dharma; the second, that one practises but becomes tired; and the third, that one doubts one's ability. The scriptures teach that all virtue follows from diligence. Even those who are not intelligent can obtain the fruit of Dharma if they are diligent. Those who are intelligent but lazy will not get the fruit − their intelligence is useless and wasted. But those who have both intelligence and diligence will have the greatest success.

5. *The perfection of meditation*

This is the perfection of meditation or concentration. Concentration must be based on an object. This is a very important practice in Dharma and even in everyday life. The Sanskrit word for concentration meditation is samatha.

If we do not look carefully, our mind seems to be quite

peaceful; but if we really look inside, it is not peaceful at all — it does not stay on the same object for a second. Our mind is like a waterfall — a continuous stream of thoughts. This constant movement prevents the mind from concentrating on an object for long. In our mind the defilements are stronger than the good qualities. We do not try to control them, and if we do, it is very difficult because we have been in the habit of following them for a very long time. Samatha means that our mind is concentrated and dwells peacefully on the object concerned. There are two kinds of meditation: discrimination meditation and concentration meditation, both of which are very important and very necessary. To remove delusion and reach the goal, we have to use both these meditations. The scriptures say that thinking and learning about Dharma is a kind of meditation. If we do not think carefully and know the nature of the object, we cannot concentrate well. The busyness of the mind is mind-produced; to quiet it, therefore, action by the mind is required — not by anything from outside. The primary action must be by the mind.

After this, factors such as a suitable place and position for meditation can be used to help. The place should be clean, quiet, close to nature, and pleasing to us. It is also helpful if the place is quiet, with good water and pure air. Our friends should be peaceful and good. The body should also be in good condition — not sick, in other words. The correct position of the body also helps. For meditation, there are seven different features of body posture.

1. If it is not painful, the vajra posture (the posture of Vajrasattva), with the legs crossed and feet resting upturned on the thighs, is best. But if it causes pain, it will distract concentration — if this is so then the left foot should be tucked under the right thigh, and the right foot should rest on the left thigh.

2. The trunk must be as straight and erect as possible within the limits of the person's physical capacity.

3. The arms should be in a bow shape, not resting against

the sides of the body, and not pushed back; they should be quite stiff. The thumbs should be level with the navel.

4. The neck should be straight and slightly inclined, with the chin in.

5. The eyes should be focused straight along the sides of the nose.

6. The mouth and lips should be relaxed, not gaping or tightly shut.

7. The tongue should be pressed — gently, not firmly — against the palate.

These are the seven elements of the vajra posture. Each is symbolic of a different stage of the path, and each also has a practical reason behind it. The crossed legs and the feet on the thighs create a locked position so that if one sits for a long time in meditation — even for months — one will not fall, being held firm. The straightness of the body is to allow the best functioning of the channels which carry the airs in our bodies, on which the mind rides. If the body is straight, these channels will not be blocked. The position of the arms is also to allow the best functioning of these channels. If one looks too high, one can easily see something distracting; if the head is too low, one gets pain in the neck and becomes sleepy. Should the mouth be too tightly closed, it will be difficult to breathe if the nose is at all blocked — but if the mouth is too widely open, the breathing will be too strong, causing high blood pressure. If the tongue is pressed against the palate, the throat and mouth will be kept moist. These are only the immediate reasons for the posture.

Just by sitting in the vajra posture, we achieve a good frame of mind, but the main work has to be done by the mind itself. The mind can be turned to deeper and higher things. It has to be used on the one hand to overcome karma (and defilements), and on the other hand to attain the virtues of a Buddha. For this, the object can only be sunyata; other meditations prepare the mind for this. If we have a very good torch which can light up anything we have to use its light to find out what is important. The root cause of all our trouble is ignorance. We have to use our knowledge of sunyata to dispel this; we must use our mind, purified by samatha and vipassana to cut the root of the tree of ignorance.

The knowledge of sunyata is essential to remove ignorance. Once we have got close to understanding sunyata completely, we are on the way to achieving

6. *The perfection of wisdom*

which is the complete comprehension of sunyata.

12   The five paths

There are five paths on which a bodhisattva develops in succession:
1. The path of equipment, gathering virtues (*sambharamarga*)
2. The path of training (*prayogamarga*)
3. The path of seeing (*darsanamarga*)
4. The path of intense contemplation (*bhavanamarga*)
5. The path of full wisdom (*vimuktimarga*)

When bodhicitta has been developed until it is natural and an intrinsic part of their being, bodhisattvas have completely attained the first path (which has lower levels before this point). They then acquire many spiritual powers, such as mental power enabling them to know other people's thoughts, to know the past and future events of other beings' lives, to fly, to multiply their bodies, and so on. Bodhisattvas are not like ordinary people who practise special techniques in order to get a particular spiritual power — these powers come naturally. But they are able to put them to good use because they help them to see the karma, spiritual development and potential of other beings, and to see whether they are in a state where they can be helped escape from samsara. They can see where they can receive teaching from the Buddhas and bodhisattvas in the various Buddha-fields. They also acquire many other virtues.

The most important thing now is for them to meditate on sunyata. When this understanding of sunyata increases they reach the second path, or training; this is the stage immediately before becoming an arya bodhisattva. They become much stronger in their meditation and spiritual powers, and can overcome even more subtle defilements.

After much meditation, they feel that their mind and sunyata are one, like water poured into water. They reach the path of seeing and become arya bodhisattvas. Their powers greatly increase and at this stage they create no new karma, although they still have their old karma and some defilements left. The bodhisattva has greater wisdom because there are fewer layers hiding reality.

The fourth and fifth paths will be explained in the next chapter.

13 *The ten levels*

There are ten levels of arya-bodhisattva:

1. The joyous (*pramudita*)
2. The stainless (*vimala*)
3. The light-maker (*prabhakari*)
4. The radiant (*arcismati*)
5. The very-hard-to-conquer (*sudurjaya*)
6. The turning-towards (*abhimukhi*)
7. The far-going (*durangama*)
8. The unshakeable (*acala*)
9. The good mind (*sadhumati*)
10. The cloud of Dharma (essence of Dharma) (*dharmamegha*)

The joyous level is reached at the third path of seeing (darsanamarga), and all the other nine at the fourth path of intense contemplation (bhavanamarga). At each level the bodhisattva acquires greater virtue and overcomes more defilements. In the scriptures, the numbers of increases in virtue are given for each level; at some levels they are innumerable. All the levels are connected, as a stream. One layer of defilements is removed at each of the first seven levels; at the eighth, the unshakeable level (acala), the remaining three layers are removed so that the bodhisattvas are nearly free from defilements. In this respect, they are equal to the lower arhats, but the virtue they have collected is much greater. These defilements are all removed by meditation on sunyata; at the eighth level there is a particular increase in the strength of this meditation. At the ninth level, the good mind (sadhumati), further defilements are removed. These are very subtle and difficult to perceive. Here, bodhisattvas are free of samsara, but their wisdom is not quite perfect. They can now recognize, and thus begin to remove, the only remaining obscuring factors. If these are not removed they cannot help beings as fully as a Buddha can. The depth to which they can help beings depends on the depth of their wisdom.

The level of the cloud of Dharma (dharmamegha) is immediately before Buddhahood, in which the last traces of defilements are worn away. The removing of obscurations is like the dispelling of increasingly fine, wispy veils. The development of greater spiritual power is like having stronger and stronger binoculars through which to see more and more clearly. At the Buddha stage all the defilements are gone. Even a small part of a Buddha's mind can see all things clearly at the same time.

At the tenth level the bodhisattvas meditate on sunyata with perfect concentration. They see it clearly and completely, but they cannot see phenomena at the same time. A Buddha can see both sunyata and phenomena at the same time. Objects *have* sunyata — emptiness of independent self-existence — but they *are not* sunyata. At the moment that this final trace of obscuration disappears, phenomenal existence suddenly appears at the same time as sunyata. At this point, Buddhas can see phenomena and sunyata simultaneously, even with their eye. This is also true for the other senses. At the time of becoming Buddhas, when the fifth path is reached, they know the deepest nature of everything, they attain the final virtue of body — they can without difficulty multiply themselves an infinite number of times — and also of speech — they have no difficulty in giving teaching to any being.

The virtue of a Buddha's speech is unlimited; if a thousand people each ask a different question in a different language at the same time, the Buddha can answer all their questions at once. We lack the inner power to do this kind of thing because of our defilements. There are other virtues to a Buddha's speech: sweetness, softness, an attraction that makes people want to listen, a quality that gives a feeling of peace to those who hear it, and so on; in all, there are sixty-four virtues of a Buddha's speech. In the various sutras can be found the different virtues of body, speech and mind; these are collected together in a work by Sakya Pandita.

There are one hundred and twelve different virtues of a Buddha's body. The duty of the Buddhas is to help beings, if it is helpful, they can multiply themselves in one second as many times as there are beings and they can manifest as any kind of being. This is always, and only, to help to free beings from samsara.

To receive this help, beings must also be in contact with the Buddha. At night, when the moon is shining on the surface of a lake which is clear and smooth, the light can shine on all parts of it; but if the surface is disturbed, the moon cannot penetrate. When it is smooth and clear, the moon is reflected clearly on it, the reflection being just like the moon in the sky. In the same way, the Buddha's help goes out to all beings equally; it is the receptivity of beings themselves that varies. Beings must, for their part, make contact with the Buddhas; otherwise they would already have taken all beings out of samsara. Buddhas have the ultimate great compassion, so they would not leave beings in suffering if they were able, by their own efforts, to free them.

The Mahayana path is the teaching of Shakyamuni, the Buddha of this present era. The Buddhas of the previous eras have not taught the Mahayana path because beings were not yet mature enough to receive the teachings.

After the historical Buddha, Shakyamuni, had finished his teaching on earth, and all the beings there at that time who had the karma to see and hear him had done so, he went to continue his work in other realms. This form is now finished, but he can still help beings in other forms. Buddhas can take everyday forms such as a friend or a guru.

Part Three
How to do the
Preliminary
Practices

1 *Refuge*

The following explanation on taking refuge is derived from an original Tibetan text; it is divided into eight different aspects:

1. Cause
2. Object
3. Time and duration
4. Method
5. Beneficial effects
6. Instructions
7. Meaning
8. Differences and their distinction

The reason for taking refuge

There may be three reasons for taking refuge: (1) out of fear; (2) out of devoted faith; (3) out of compassion. In this present life, we all experience fear. We may be frightened of enemies, evil spirits or demons who want to do us harm. We may be frightened of rebirth in the hell regions, or we may simply be scared of samsara in general.

The object of refuge

Refuge is taken in the guru as well as the Three Jewels. The guru is our kind teacher, guiding us on the path to enlightenment.

Buddha, the noble saint, rid himself of all bad deeds and failings and, hence, attained all virtues. He taught the holy

Dharma, which is the only way to free ourselves from our deep-rooted ignorance.

The Sangha is the holy community of sravakas and bodhisattvas who have adopted and practised the method. We devotedly take refuge in these Three Jewels and the guru.

The time and duration of taking refuge

One takes refuge from now until the essence of enlightenment, Buddhahood, is attained.

The method

The quality of the object of refuge must first be completely understood, until deep faith is established in the Buddha, who is our teacher, in the Dharma path and in the sangha.

The five beneficial effects

Choosing the wrong object of refuge results in impure karma. However, by taking proper refuge, which is the basis of all morality, this can be purified. We are then accepted and integrated as a member of the holy community, the sangha, thus receiving the protection of a personal protector.

Without taking refuge, no true moral conduct is possible. As it says in the *Abhidharmakosa*: There is not a single person out of those who perform religious duties, who has not taken refuge! In the *skyabs-ksum-bdun-cu-pa* it says: Taking refuge is the basis of all Dharma practice!

Taking refuge gives protection against irritating influences coming either from human beings or from evil spirits.

Refuge has always been taken in all kinds of divinities, such as Isvara, Brahma and others. By taking refuge in the Three Jewels, karmic impurities resulting from the wrong choice of refuge will be cleansed.

Those who take refuge in the Three Jewels become Buddhists.

Those who take refuge in the teaching method will be protected by the divine guardians.

The general meaning of the two instructions

There is a distinction between ordinary and special instructions:

Ordinary instructions. By listening to oral instructions, the proper preconditions for the achievement of various spiritual stages are produced. With great respect for the guru, one listens to his Dharma teaching. One turns one's mind towards the most supreme spiritual spheres, which lead to a harmonious Dharma practice. This entails the following four directives: (1) one must control one's mind; (2) one must exercise love and compassion for all living beings; (3) one should make offerings to the Three Jewels; and (4) one should attach great value to one's religious vows and abide by their rules.

Those who take refuge in the Buddha have become Buddhists and should not take refuge in non-Buddhist deities. By taking refuge in the holy Dharma, they are protected against demonic influences. If they also take refuge in the holy Sangha, then they should not adopt other religious teachings.

Special instructions. One should make the ordinary as well as the special offerings and when one is about to eat any food one should first present it as an offering.

One should not take the name of the Three Jewels in vain, either to save life or to benefit oneself in any way.

Wherever one goes, one should take refuge. Whatever illness may occur, one should take refuge in the Three Jewels.

One should worship the Buddhas and respect all their images.

One should pay reverence to the holy Dharma teaching and respect every word that has been written.

One should pay great respect to the holy sangha.

The meaning of taking refuge

Taking refuge is an effective shield against fear and anxiety in this life and it also protects against fear of rebirth in the hell regions. Taking refuge is an overall protection against samsaric fear.

The Mahayana path offers greater protection than the Hinayana path. In the *Uttaratantra* we read as follows: Taking refuge is an essential practice of the Hinayana, Mahayana and Vajrayana paths. It protects against all misfortunes and unfavourable conditions. It saves us from the lower realms.

The four main distinctions of taking refuge

There are a number of attributes to taking refuge, which are based on several factors. The object of refuge will also influence its results. There are also various different reasons for taking refuge:

The sravakas and pratyekas take refuge out of faith. In the Mahayana path refuge is taken out of great compassion.

The result or fruit of taking refuge depends on the object of refuge. For example, the sravaka strives for arhathood and takes refuge in the Sangha. The pratyeka longs to understand the interdependent development of all things and therefore takes refuge in the Dharma. A follower of the Mahayana path strives for Buddhahood, thus taking refuge in the Buddha.

As mentioned before, refuge lasts until Buddhahood is finally reached.

The sravakas and pratyekas take refuge for their own benefit.

How to perform the actual practice

Seated in the proper meditation posture (see pages 81–82) begin by reflecting on the four common foundations: the difficulties of obtaining favourable conditions for the practice of Dharma, the impermanence of life, the truth of the law of cause and effect and the faults or unsatisfactoriness of existence (samsara). These four are necessary in order to

produce a firm basis for engaging in the actual practice of
Dharma rather than just performing the external rituals. By
thinking in this way induce upon your mind's continuum
sadness and renunciation.

Now, bring to mind the kindness of all sentient beings –
your past mothers – and out of love and compassion cultivate the desire to practise the path in order to obtain Buddhahood for the sake of sentient beings. With this motivation and a good understanding of the eight aspects of refuge,
go for refuge in the following manner reciting the words and
performing the visualization conjunctly without any mental
distractions:

> The impure vision of subject and object dissolves
> into emptiness. From this state arises a ground
> made entirely of sapphire (vaidurya) gems, shaded
> blue, with bright golden patterns. In the centre of
> this is a lake of nectar beautified with trees and
> flowers and emanation birds singing sweet sounds
> of the holy Dharma. Above the lake is a rainbow
> tent, sweet-smelling, adorned with a rainfall of va-
> rious heavenly flowers and complete with all the
> adornments of a pure realm. In the centre is a
> wish-fulfilling tree arising from the self-perceived
> transcendental knowledge adorned with leaves,
> flowers and fruit: just remembering it grants all
> wishes. On the tree is a vari-coloured, four-petalled
> lotus, in the centre of which is a jewelled lion
> throne with a lotus, sun and moon placed one on
> top of the other.
>
> Seated on this is one's own root guru, combina-
> tion of all the Buddhas, indistinguishable from Va-
> jradhara, the master of all the races, his body blue
> in colour with one face and two hands holding
> vajra and bell crossed at his heart. He is adorned
> with jewel and bone ornaments and wears vari-
> coloured silk garments. Some of his dark blue hair

is piled on his head, the rest hangs beautifully. His two feet are in the vajra posture, thus he appears in the sambhogakaya form. He is very happy and smiling and faces towards you.

Surrounding him, seated in clockwise order and starting from the front are the lineage gurus, all in the form of Vajradhara.

On the front petal are the deities of the four tantras. On the right petal are all the Buddhas in their nirmanakaya and sambhogakaya forms. On the back petal are holy scriptures, piled up like a mountain. On the left petal are bodhisattvas in lay and ordained forms, inconceivable in number. In addition, other gurus, deities, Buddhas and bodhisattvas, sravakas, pratyekabuddhas, viras, dakinis, dharmapalas, wealth deities and all other suitable objects of refuge should be imagined filling the sky like a cluster of clouds.

On the ground in front of this are seated oneself, parents, and all sentient beings of the six realms in the form of human beings.

This visualization of the objects of refuge is both complex and highly symbolic. The place of meditation, for example, is visualized as a Buddha-land complete with bodhisattvas emanating in the form of birds, and a wish-fulfilling tree arising out of the Buddha's vision. The jewelled throne on the wish-fulfilling tree signifies that the one seated upon it can bestow all wishes. The lotus on the throne symbolizes that just as a lotus born from the mud rises beautifully from the impurity, so the one seated on the lotus is untainted by the faults of samsara. The sun disc shows that just as the sun ripens fruits and crops, so the mind is ripened by the benevolent warmth of the guru. The moon disc symbolizes that just as the light of the moon is cooling, similarly the heat of the afflictions is cooled by the kindness of the guru. The blue colour of Vajradhara's body — in whose form the root guru is visualized – represents the unchangeable nature of the dharmadhatu. Having one face indicates that all dharmas in suchness are of one taste. The two hands represent relative truth and ultimate truth; being crossed at the heart symbolizes that both truths are needed in order to attain Buddhahood. The five-pronged golden vajra in the right hand represents the nature of the five transcendental wisdoms. The sound of the bell held in the left hand represents the sound of emptiness. The eight jewel ornaments represent the noble eight-fold path. The six ornaments of bone represent the Buddhas of the six races. The two feet in the vajra posture represent the transcendence of the two extremes of samsara and nirvana.

Surrounding the root guru are the lineage gurus of the Lam Dre Tshok Shay teaching (see pages 102–103) – the principal teaching upheld by the Sakya tradition – also appearing in the form of Vajradhara and seated on moon discs.

On the front petal of the lotus are the deities of the four classes of tantra. An example of kriya tantra deities are the three bodhisattvas Avalokitesvara, Manjushri and Vajrapani. An example of a carya tantra deity is Manjushri Arapaca. An example of a yoga tantra deity is Mahavairocana (Sarvavidya). Examples of anuttarayoga tantra deities are Hevajra, Cakrasamvara and Guhyasamaja.

On the back petal are scriptures in Tibetan design, the labelled end pointing towards oneself, and the sounds of Dharma ceaselessly pouring out.

Surrounding the tree are other lineage gurus as well as wealth dieties who are bodhisattvas on various stages, and viras and dakinis who are male and female emanations of the Buddhas in nirmanakaya form.

In front of this assembly of the objects of refuge you visualize yourself seated with father and other male relatives on the right side, mother and other female relatives on the left side, all enemies and evil spirits in the form of human beings in front, and all sentient beings of the six realms of existence in the form of human beings behind. Then, with one voice and one intention, imagine that all the sentient beings visualized around you go for refuge until reaching enlightenment with full faith that the Triple Gem is the only hope for gaining liberation, full reliance on the Triple Gem as the most excellent refuge and full respect of body, speech and mind, reciting the following prayer:

> In the most holy guru who is the essence of the qualities and deeds of the body, speech and mind of all the tathagatas abiding in the ten directions and three times, the source of the eighty-four thousand Dharmas and master of the arya Sangha, I and all sentient beings equal to the ends of space, from this time forth until the essence of enlightenment is reached, steadfastly take refuge. I take refuge in my venerable root guru and in the holy masters of the lineage, I take refuge in the blessed accomplished Buddhas, I take refuge in the holy Dharma, I take refuge in the arya Sangha.

If you intend to recite the refuge prayer one hundred thousand times as a practice, recite:

> I take refuge in the venerable, holy gurus, I take refuge in the blessed accomplished Buddhas, I take refuge in the holy Dharma, I take refuge in the arya Sangha.

Having recited the four-line refuge prayer as many times as possible make prayers to the guru and Triple Gem. Then, to conclude the session, fold your hands together at the heart and recite:

> To the guru and the Three Precious Gems I bow down and go for refuge. May you bless my mind's continuum.

If you wish you may also recite:

> To the guru and the Three Precious Gems I bow down and go for refuge. May you bless the body,

speech and mind of myself and all sentient beings.
Bless my mind to proceed in the Dharma. Bless me
to practise successfully the holy Dharma. Bless me
to allay the errors of the path. Bless me that the
illusive vision may appear as the dharmadhatu.
Bless me to stop irreligious thoughts. Bless me to
produce love and compassion. Bless me to practise
the two bodhicittas. Bless me to attain Buddhahood
quickly.

Then visualize the following:

From the objects of refuge, various coloured light
rays issue forth touching oneself and others, purifying the two obscurations along with their residues,
completely accomplishing the two accumulations.
The bodies of each become pure rainbow bodies,
the mind of each becomes the dharmakaya and they
depart to the individual Buddha realms. The surrounding objects of refuge dissolve into light and
absorb into the guru who dissolves from top to
bottom into a ball of blue light rays at the heart,
bright as the sun. This enters through the top of
your head blessing your mind's continuum.

When the light rays issue from the objects of refuge visualize
that they completely purify all the obscurations of the afflictions (desire, hatred, ignorance, and so on) and of knowables
(all the thoughts connected with subject, object and their
interdependence) of oneself and all other sentient beings.
Also, the two accumulations of merit and wisdom (that is,
the realization of emptiness) needed for the attainment of
Buddhahood are accomplished. The ordinary, impure bodies
of each sentient being are purified becoming clear and made
of light, similar in nature to a rainbow.

When the guru dissolves into you blessing your mind
think:

The clear aspect of the mind is Sangha, the empty

aspect is the holy Dharma, the combination of the two is the Buddha, its nature which is the non-differentiation of these three is the guru.

Meditate as long as possible on the firm conviction of the nature and three aspects of the mind that represent the ultimate guru and the Triple Gem. When one examines the mind, nothing can be found, but at the same time there is a continuity of mind, this continuity is the clear aspect. When one examines this clear mind, again nothing can be found, no colour, shape and so on, this is the empty aspect. Just as fire and the heat of fire are inseparable, so the clear and empty aspects of mind are inseparable, this is the combination of the two.

At this point, one can recite the prayer for developing bodhicitta, the enlightenment thought, the extraordinary cause of accomplishing Buddhahood:

I must attain complete enlightenment for the sake of liberating from existence all living beings who have been my mothers, for this purpose I am practising the profound path of all the Buddhas.

If possible the prayer should be recited one hundred thousand times.

At the end of each session seal the virtues with a dedication prayer.

By this virtue may all beings accomplish the accumulations of merit and transcendental knowledge and obtain the two holy bodies which arise from merit and transcendental knowledge.

If you wish to practise the refuge and prostrations (see pages 105 – 108) simultaneously perform one prostration for each recitation of the four-line refuge prayer.

2 Prostration

This explanation of the profound meaning of prostration originates from the great Mahasiddha Kyun Phobha. The explanations have been collected and written down by Sakya Pandita, who was an emanation of Arya Manjushri.

There are seven elements to prostration, and one must prostrate through the three doors of body, speech and mind.

Before we prostrate it is essential to develop the enlightenment thought, bodhicitta, by reciting the prayer of taking refuge at least three times. During the recitation of the prayer, we should visualize the guru, the Buddha, the Dharma and the Sangha, and make offerings to them.

Firstly, we can offer material things. This type of offering is to be made in a specific order. First, we should offer a bowl of water: by this offering we supply drinking water for the holy object. Secondly, we offer another bowl of water, in order to purify our own ignorance. Thirdly, we offer flowers, the symbol of great compassion. The fourth offering is incense, which symbolizes morality. The fifth offering is light, for instance a butterlamp symbolizing the light of wisdom. The sixth offering is a bowl of water perfumed with saffron. The seventh offering is food, symbolizing the spiritual nourishment of samadhi. We can also offer the sounds of instruments. These sounds symbolize the sound of Dharma that awakens the mind.

The second kind of offering is spiritual. With this type of offering we should visualize the object that we wish to offer. We can offer spiritually by visualizing the offering, as did

Buddha Samantabhadra, who made offerings as vast as space. By virtue of this kind of offering all ignorance is purified.

We then confess all the sins that have been accumulated in our previous lives and in this present life so that they can be purified.

We should rejoice in the virtuous deeds which the Buddhas and bodhisattvas perform for the benefit of all sentient beings.

We should request that the Buddhas, bodhisattvas and spiritual leaders remain until the end of samsara.

We should pray to the Buddhas and bodhisattvas that they will teach all sentient beings and spread the holy Dharma.

We should share the merit that we have accumulated and dedicate it to the attainment of Buddhahood for all sentient beings.

Another type of offering is to offer the universe to Buddha.

A short wishing prayer

> All sins and disrespectful deeds, especially those directed towards my guru, originate from a wrong vision. May these impure actions be purified and transformed into pure thought.
> When respectful towards my guru, all virtuous thoughts will come effortlessly.
> All inner and outer obstacles shall be eliminated and transformed through blessing.
> By the virtue of prostrating to this holy object, may I and all sentient beings be purified.

How to prostrate

You should stand up straight, facing the guru and Triple Gem, and concentrate deeply on bodhicitta.

The palms of the hands should be pressed together, with

the fingers directed upwards, in front of the heart. The right hand symbolizes wisdom and the left hand symbolizes the method — compassion. By this gesture our path joins method and wisdom.

Then the hands are placed on top of the head. This gesture symbolizes our wish to be reborn in Sukhavati, the peaceful and pure Buddha-land.

Put the hands in front of the forehead. This symbolizes the purification of all physical defilements.

Put the hands in front of the throat. This purifies the defilements of wrong speech.

Put the hands in front of the heart again, thus purifying the defilements of the mind, such as impure thoughts.

Separate the hands. This symbolizes the activity of the sambhogakaya.

With feet together, kneel down. This symbolizes the gradual attainment of the five paths and ten bodhisattva levels.

Press the forehead to the earth. This symbolizes the wish to attain the eleventh bodhisattva level.

The action of kneeling and the gesture of the hands symbolize the four virtuous activities.

During the prostration, the main nadi (the subtle channel that runs the length of the spine) bends. With this bending, all knots are undone and the energy can flow freely.

The spine should be kept straight, thus allowing air to flow freely through the kundalini. As we rise again, we are symbolically freed from the sufferings of samsara, we arise to a state of liberation.

This is an explanation of the physical action and mental attitudes to be observed in order to practise a truly beneficial prostration. The benefits of this virtuous practice are many. First, we are freed from the sufferings of samsara. We are liberated. There are also many benefits in this life.

Our life will be long, we will be free from illness and our wishes will be fulfilled. Through strong wishing and a powerful intention, we can reach the pure Buddha-land and

Buddhahood in a future incarnation. Through the limitless virtue of prostration, the precious and holy thoughts of the Buddhas and bodhisattvas will reach all sentient beings.

When we share the merits we have acquired after having prostrated, we should recite:

> With my heart going out in all ten directions where the supreme jewel-like Dharma has declined or not yet spread, moved by the powerful force of great mercy, through my virtue may it expose the great treasure, bringing pleasure and aid. By the merit that has been accumulated by the practice of this virtue, my prayer is that this merit may increase and result in the attainment of Buddhahood for all sentient beings.

By the virtue of the prostrations, the practice of hearing the Dharma, contemplating its meaning and meditation are strongly developed. All sentient beings, who have been our kind mothers, will be freed from their suffering and will attain Buddhahood as soon as possible. All sentient beings receive the blessing of the gurus and the Three Jewels.

3 *The mandala offering*

The main purpose of offering the mandala is the accumulation of merit. There are two kinds of merit. The first is the material way of accumulating merit, by offering to a holy object. People like joy and happiness and they tend to think that wealth will bring these to them. By practising this method one will become wealthier, but the most important result is an increase in inner wealth, which is the cause of great peace. This is the result of the elimination of ignorance.

This practice consists of offering our own wealth and material possessions, but they are not nearly enough in view of the tremendously precious blessings of the gurus, Buddhas and bodhisattvas. Therefore we transform all our wealth and material possessions into a completely pure universe which we then offer. In fact even this is not sufficient to repay the conquerors for their immense kindness in bestowing upon us their blessings and showing us the path leading towards liberation. By receiving these blessings and teachings of wisdom all our suffering will be allayed. Our ignorance will be purified and transformed, and we will be freed from samsaric existence. An understanding of these processes can also be gained by people with scientific knowledge. They can also come to an understanding of some of the basic underlying patterns of our universe. If our accumulation of merit is not strong, we will not be able to truly develop our minds.

The second way of accumulating merit is of even greater importance as it entails an inner method. Its main element is the development of a powerful sense of love and compassion. In the practice of Buddhism we generally offer water bowls, but by an inner transformation of the offering we come to hear the vast ocean of Dharma. Our inner knowledge is like a fully blossomed flower from which clear light shines forth. By this method we merely offer the mental stabilization of samadhi.

In the practice of Buddhism we habitually offer the sound of instruments; by this method we transform the outer sound into an inner sound of Dharma which wakens us from our ignorant and slumbering state of mind.

These preliminary practices are of supreme importance for the practitioner as it is not possible to make any progress along the path to liberation while the accumulated merit is still poor. Buddha Shakyamuni has therefore shown us by example, mainly by performing the twelve miracles. The first of these simply comprises the accumulation of merit. It was through his vast accumulation of merit that he was able to eliminate all obscurations and defilements, whereby he attained full enlightenment.

How to make a mandala offering

In order to accomplish the accumulation of merit, the offering of the mandala is performed. On a raised area, set the shrine mandala, with five heaps of rice and around it starting with the two water offerings (and going in a clockwise direction) arrange the offerings. In front of you place the offering mandala. If the mandala is made of a precious metal such as gold or silver, then it should not be smaller in diameter than the distance between the tips of your outstretched thumb and middle finger, that is, about six inches. If the mandala is made of an inferior material, such as brass or steel, then it must be less in diameter than the distance between one's elbow and outstretched middle finger, that is, about eighteen inches. Although it is described like this, in practice, since one is offering to a pure realm regardless of whether it is a superior or an inferior material, it is important to choose the larger and wider ones. This was said by my precious guru, Ngawang Lekpa Rinpoche. Concerning the material used for heaps, the best is the powder made from jewels; the next best are various herbs; the inferior kind are different grains. The grains must first be washed to remove all dirt and dust, leaving it quite clean. You should obtain Kashmiri or Nepalese saffron and soak it in water to make scented water to put on the mandala.

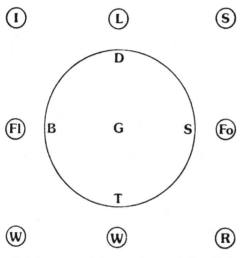

This is the shrine mandala, together with the offerings. On the mandala are placed five heaps of rice; G in the centre represents the guru; T in front, the tutelary deities; B on the right, the Buddhas; D behind, the Dharma; and S on the left, the Sangha. The offerings placed around the mandala starting from the front and going in a clockwise direction, are: W, drinking water; W, washing water; Fl, flowers; I, incense; L, lamp; S, scented water; Fo, food, and R, rice, which is there just to fill in that blank space which is known as 'direction holder.'

Having recited the prayer of refuge and bodhicitta as described earlier, purify all impure visions into emptiness by reciting the following mantra: OM SVABHAWA SHUDDHAH SARVADHARMAH SVABHAWA SHUDDHO HANG. Then:

From BHRUM arises a jewelled celestial mansion in the centre of which is a lion-supported throne, lotus, sun and moon placed one upon another. Upon that is one's venerable guru in the form of Vajradhara. He is beautifully adorned with the major and minor marks of a Buddha and is very happy and smiling. He is surrounded by the lineage gurus. In front of him are the tutelary deities, on the right the Buddhas, behind the holy Dharma, and on the left the Sangha. In addition, like a vast cluster of clouds are other places of refuge

Light rays issue from the hearts of each of these, invoking from Buddha realms in the ten directions countless conquerors along with their Sons who fill the sky. Then each object of refuge is absorbed into its respective form — thus the samaya aspect and jnana aspect are nondually merged.

Now imagine that from your heart countless offering goddesses issue forth, filling the sky in order to make offerings.

OM GURU BUDDHA BODHISATTVA SAPARIWARA ARGHAM PADYAM PUSHPE DHUPE ALOKE GHANDHE NAIWIDYE SHABDA AH HUM.

Then you should recite the dharani of the cloud of offering once:

OM NAMO BHAGAWATE VAJRA SARA PRAMARDANE TATHAGATAYA ARHATE SAMYAKSAMBUDDHAYA TADYATHA OM VAJRE VAJRE MAHATEJAVAJRE MAHAVIDYAVAJRE MAHABODHICITTAVAJRE MAHABODHI-MANDOPASAMKRAMANA VAJRE SARVAKARMA AWARANA VISHODHANA VAJRA SVAHA

Next, you should recite the seven fold prayer, in its brief form, as follows:

I prostrate to the holy place of refuge; I offer a cloud of offerings like that of Samantabhadra; I confess all sins and downfalls accumulated since beginningless time; I rejoice in all the merits of virtuous deeds; I request the conquerors along with their children to turn the wheel of Dharma; I entreat those conquerors to remain and not pass into nirvana; I dedicate the accumulation of virtue for sentient beings to obtain enlightenment.

If you feel like it, it is good to recite the seven fold prayer, found in the prayer of Samantabhadra, as given below:

As many as there are in the worlds of the ten directions, all the tathagatas of the three times, the lions amongst humans, to all of them, without exception, I bow, with sincerity of body, voice and mind. By the power of this prayer of good actions, do I, bowing with as many bodies as atoms in the Buddha realms, before all the conquerors manifest in my mind, fully prostrate to all the victorious ones. On each single atom as many Buddhas as atoms, seated in the midst of their children, so all the Dharma realms, without exception, I imagine filled with the victorious ones. With unending oceans of praises for them, with all the sounds of an ocean of various tones, I fully extol all the conquerors' virtues, and praise all the sugatas. With fine blossoms and fine garlands, sweet sounds and balms and choice canopies, the choicest lamps and finest incense, I make offerings to those conquerors. With fine garments and choice fragrances, sandalwood powders equalling Mount Sumeru, and all the choicest, most special arrangements, I make offerings to those conquerors. Whatever offerings are incomparable, vast in imagination, I profer those to all conquerors; by the powers of my faith in good actions I bow to and worship all the victorious ones. Whatever sins I have perpetrated through the power of desire, hatred and delusion, by body, voice and mind as well, each one of those

I confess. I rejoice in whatever merits of the victorious ones exist in the ten directions, and I rejoice
in the merits of the Buddha's Sons, of pratyekabuddhas, sravakas and all sentient beings. They
who are the lights of the worlds of the ten directions, winners of the non-clinging awakening on
the enlightened stage, to all those protectors I offer
entreaties to turn the incomparable wheel of the
Dharma. To those who wish to manifest the passing from sorrow, I fervently pray, with clasped
palms, to stay for aeons, as many as the Buddha
realm's atoms, for the benefit and welfare of all
sentient beings. Whatever little merit I have gathered
through prostrating, offering, confessing, rejoicing,
requesting, and praying, for the sake of enlightenment, all this I dedicate.

Having taken up the offering mandala in your left hand,
take some grains with the fingers of your right hand. While
reciting the one-hundred syllable mantra of Vajrasattva,
clean the mandala with the right wrist until it is clear of dust
and dirt. Think that all the sins, obscurations, faults and
failings upon your mind's continuum are purified. Place a
few drops of scented water upon the mandala and spread it
over the entire surface with your fingers. If you offer a dry
mandala, then you will be reborn in a very dry place and
your mind's continuum will be devoid of the moisture of
compassion. Therefore, it is necessary to apply scented water, since faults such as these will arise.

The manner of placing the heaps of grain should be learnt
directly from a teacher, according to the living tradition.
Nowadays it is usual for people to let the grains fall through
the space where the small finger touches the palm, in placing
the heaps. Since proceeding in this manner is disrespectful to
the Triple Gem, they should be placed by allowing the
grains to pass through the tips of the five fingers. The central
heap should be high, while the surrounding ones are lower.
If you make the heaps too large around the edge of the

mandala, then in the next life you will be born in an uncivilized place. Also, if you make the heaps so big that they mix together, you will have an inner element illness and there will be the problem of disagreement between the teacher and his disciples; thus, be careful. My venerable guru told me again and again that it is very important to be careful, since many great, important omens will arise in accordance with the way one offers the mandala. In the beginning, you should lead with the recitation of the thirty-seven heap mandala once, and then the counting should be done with the seven heap mandala.

The nature of the mandala is your own body, wealth and virtuous deeds accumulated in the three times and those of others. The cause is its formation from various jewels. The form is Mount Sumeru, the four continents, sun and moon, which emanate from the mind a hundred million-fold; from each of these sets issue forth millions of light rays, and upon the tip of each of these light rays are countless sets of worlds of four continents. All of these pure realms, the containers, wholly possess the ten worldly virtuous qualities, (that is, house earth, field earth, house wood, fuel wood, drinking water, field water, house stone, grinding stone, grass near the house, and grass far from the house), and all the sentient beings living in them, the contained, wholly possess the special basis of all the eighteen favourable conditions for the practice of Dharma (that is, the eight freedoms and the ten endowments), the special basis of the seven qualities of higher realms (that is, they possess lineage of family, physical beauty, health, wealth, wisdom, power, are devoid of sickness, and possess long life), and the four great conditions (that is, dwelling in a suitable place, relying upon the holy ones, having religiously applied oneself in former lives, and having collected merit). Also, they are all of the Mahayana lineage and have keen sense-organs. Having visualized the worlds as filled with these kinds of people, you make offering. You must hold these with the view that they are like an illusion without truth, not existing in their own nature (that is, the world of the mandala is there, but untrue like the image in a mirror, or a mirage). It is difficult to obtain great benefits if you accumulate a hundred thousand offerings by just reciting the words and placing the grain on top of the circular mandala but without proper visualization − thus it is said. In accordance with the tradition of former Sakya lamas, venerable Lama Rinpoche (Ngawang Lekpa) offered with hand and mouth − that is, correctly offered − the seven heap mandala one million times. If you are unable to do that, then having offered the seven heap mandala as many times as possible, recite shorter mandala offerings such as 'Sa zhi po ...' (This has a base of earth, etc.) or 'Zhing kham nam par ...' (here is a pure spiritual realm, etc.) together with counting.

The thirty-seven heap mandala offering

OM VAJRA BHUMI AH HUM

The universe is wholly pure, of great power, with earth of gold.

OM VAJRA REKHE AH HUM

The outermost limit of the universe is surrounded with an iron fence, and in the centre is the HUM.

Here is the king of mountains, Mount Sumeru, the eastern continent of Purvavideha, the southern continent of Jambudvipa, the western continent of Aparagodaniya, the northern continent of Uttarakuru, Deha and Videha, Camara and Aparacamara, Satha and Uttaramantrina, Kurava and Kaurava, the treasure mountains, wish-fulfilling trees, wish-fulfilling cows, unploughed harvests, precious wheels, precious jewels, precious queens, precious ministers, precious elephants, precious excellent horses, precious generals, vases of great treasure, goddessess of beauty, goddesses of garlands, goodesses of song, goddesses of dance, goddesses of incense, goddesses of flowers, goddesses of lamps, goddesses of perfume, sun, moon, precious umbrellas, banners of victory. This most perfect offering of the wealth of gods and humans, to the greatly kind root guru and the lineage gurus who are glorious and holy, to the deities in the mandalas of the tutelary deities, to the Buddhas and bodhisattvas, to the protectors who guard the holy Dharma, and to the powerful gods of wealth, I offer. Through compassion, please accept it for the sake of living beings; having accepted it, please bestow your blessings. Having accepted it, please bless the arising of the complete accomplishment of the two accumulations of merit and transcendental knowledge upon my mind's continuum; bless me that the two obscurations along with all residues may be purified and cleansed, bless me that the special samadhi of the two stages may be produced upon my mind's continuum, please bless me that I may attain the holy stage of the two bodies of a Buddha.

How to offer the thirty-seven heap mandala

Holding the mandala in the left hand, take some grain between the thumb and forefinger of the right hand and wipe clean the top of the mandala with the wrist of the right hand very thoroughly, taking some time over it. If any bit of dirt remains on the mandala, so are we unable to clear away the afflictions and obscurations from our mind. If it is made very clean, so we rid ourselves of the two obscurations. (So, even though the mandala may not be dirty, we wipe it carefully to purify the mind.) While cleaning the mandala, we should imagine that we are cleaning away all the sins, unhappiness and obscurations of all beings, and at the same time recite the one-hundred syllable mantra of Vajrasattva. In this way, body, speech and mind each have their own work.

The world of the mandala is similar to this world we inhabit, but not the same. The world we live in is the product of the common karma of all beings, and the world of the mandala is a new world, and a real world, the embodiment of the real merit, wealth and body – past, present and future – of those who make the offering. Make the mandala offering with an unified effort of the three doors of body, speech and mind by making the heaps with the body, uttering the words with the voice and visualizing the arising of the object of meditation with the mind.

First, laying down the grain that you have in your hand, pour a little scented water onto the mandala. Then once again pick up some grain. Then, as you recite 'OM VAJRA BHUMI, etc.' with the second and middle fingers of the right hand, beginning at the centre, draw a line to the north-east and then a continuous line should be drawn in order to make a square (that is, from north-east to south-east to south-west to north-west and finally back to the north-east. Where the Buddha dwells is the east. At this time, he is in front of you, so the first line you draw will be a diagonal to your left and away from yourself, that is to a point on the Buddha's right). At the same time, imagine that below the earth base mandala is a water mandala and below that is an air mandala. These three mandalas are the same in circumference, but the air mandala is twice as deep as the water mandala and this water mandala in turn is twice as deep as the earth mandala. Also, at this time, you should not be thinking of the instruments that you are using, but you should see all this as a truly created world. In this way, you keep the three doors acting in unison.

Next, as you recite 'OM VAJRA REKHE, etc.,' draw a line around the circumference of the mandala, starting and finishing at the north-east and moving in a clockwise direction. At this point, imagine a circle of metal – iron mountains arising on top of the earth mandala – bounding the circumference. Then place the grains in your hand in the centre of the mandala, with the words, 'in the centre is a HUM' and visualize that the letter HUM, blue in colour, arises there.

At the words 'King of Mountains, Mount Sumeru', visualize this mountain arising in the centre of the mandala, in the centre of a vast sea. It is ringed at the base with four terraces. The eastern side is made of diamonds, white in colour; the southern of blue sapphire; the western of red ruby; and the northern of yellow gold. Mount Sumeru is encircled by seven separate bands of golden mountains, square in shape, and outside these the four continents are situated, one on each side. Beyond these again are the iron mountains of the outer limit. Between the continents and the golden mountain-bands, between each of the bands and between the golden mountains and Mount Sumeru, and also between the outer limits and the four continents is sea. Mount Sumeru, the mountains and the four continents all have their foundations on the earth mandala; there is no sea beneath them. The uppermost terrace of Mount Sumeru and the innermost square band of golden mountains are both half as high as the summit of the King of Mountains. The second band of golden mountains is half as high as the innermost, the third half as high as the second and so on. The sea between the innermost band and Mount Sumeru is twice as wide as that between the second and first band, which in turn is twice as wide as that between the third and second. (1)

Uttering the words 'the eastern continent of Purvavideha,' place grains on the eastern point of the mandala and imagine a great white continent, made of diamonds and semi-circular in shape. (2)

Uttering the words 'the southern continent of Jambudvipa,' place grains on the southern point of the mandala and imagine the great blue continent, made of sapphire and trapezoidal in shape. (3)

Uttering the words 'the western continent of Aparagodaniya,' place grains on the western point of the mandala and imagine a great red continent, made of ruby and circular in shape. (4)

Uttering the words 'the northern continent of Uttarakuru' place grains on the northern point of the mandala and imagine a great yellow continent, made of gold and sqaure in shape. (5)

The two sub-continents placed on either side of the main continent should be visualized as half the size of the main one, of the same colour, shape and element as the main one also. When placing heaps of grain at either side of the main continent, utter the name of each of the minor continents. (6–13)

Next, utter the words 'the treasure mountains,' and place a heap in the east below the eastern continent and imagine that the three eastern continents are covered by many high mountains, made of jewels and very beautiful. (14)

Uttering 'wish-fulfilling trees' in the south, imagine that the three southern continents are thickly wooded with jewelled trees, extremely beautiful, with their trunks, branches, leaves and flowers all made of different jewels and precious substances. (15)

Uttering 'wish-fulfilling cows' in the west, imagine that in the three western continents are many beautiful cows, with blue, jewel-like horns and hooves. All material things that can be desired issue from each hair of these animals' hides. (16)

Uttering 'unploughed harvests' in the north, imagine that fine crops are growing in the three northern continents; although the land has not been ploughed and no seed has been sown, crops grow spontaneously. The crops are harvested again and again, and immediately afterwards the fields are full of ripened crops again. (17)

Uttering 'precious wheels' place a heap in the eastern section of the mandala and imagine that the sky above the eastern countries is filled with countless precious wheels, made of gold, each with a thousand spokes. (18)

Uttering 'precious jewels,' place a heap in the south and imagine that the southern sky if filled with countless precious jewels. From these fall showers of objects which satisfy all desires, while their great radiance illuminates all the surrounding countries and a beneficial influence emanates from them, which can cure all illnesses. (19)

Uttering 'precious queens,' place a heap in the western section of the mandala and imagine that the western sky is

filled with countless precious queens. The queens possess
many great qualities, including beauty, a touch which can be
of any nature desired by the emperor, no envy, and so on.
(20)

Uttering 'precious ministers,' place a heap in the northern
part of the mandala and imagine that in the northern sky
there are countless precious ministers who have the power
to execute without fail any order of the emperor in accordance with the Dharma, and also to perceive treasure hidden
under the ground. (21)

Uttering 'precious elephants,' place a heap in the south-
east and imagine that the sky in that region is filled with
countless great white precious elephants resembling snow-
mountains, possessed of the knowledge of movement, with
the power to overcome all enemies. (22)

Uttering 'precious excellent horses,' place a heap in the
south-west and imagine that the sky of that region is filled
with countless precious horses, called 'all-knowing,' able to
go round the whole world in half a day, and knowing how
to do whatever their master may desire. (23)

Uttering 'precious generals,' place a heap in the north-
west – and imagine that in the sky of that region are
countless precious generals, able to overcome all enemies
without harming them. (24)

Uttering 'vases of great treasure,' place a heap in the
north-east and imagine that in the skies of that region are
countless treasure vases. From these any wealth that may be
desired can be obtained. Fine scarves are wrapped around
their necks, and in their mouths are arranged the jewelled
branches of precious trees. (25)

Uttering 'goddesses of beauty', place a heap in the south-
east and imagine that in the sky of that region are countless
goddesses of beauty, white in colour, and holding a vajra in
each hand. Their arms are held akimbo and placed on their
hips. (26)

Uttering 'goddesses of garlands,' place a heap in the
south-west and imagine that in the sky of that region are
countless goddesses of garlands, yellow in colour, and hold-

ing garlands of flowers in their hands which are raised to their foreheads. (27)

Uttering 'goddesses of song,' place a heap in the north-west and imagine that in the sky of that region are countless goddesses of song, white and red in colour, and holding a *piwang* (guitar-like instrument) in their hands. (28)

Uttering 'goddesses of dance,' place a heap in the north-east and visualize that in the sky of that region are countless goddesses of dance, green in colour, and dancing with a vajra in each hand. (29)

Uttering 'goddesses of incense,' place a heap in the south-east and visualize that countless goddessess of incense appear on the outer mountains of that region, white in colour, and holding a vase of incense. (30)

Uttering 'goddesses of flowers,' place a heap in the south-west and visualize that countless goddesses of flowers appear on the outer mountains of that region, yellow in colour, and holding vases of flowers. (31)

Uttering 'goddesses of lamps,' place a heap in the north-west and visualize that countless goddesses of lamps appear on the outer mountains of that region, red and white in colour, and holding lamps. (32)

Uttering 'goddesses of perfume,' place a heap in the north-east and visualize that countless goddesses of perfume appear on the outer mountains of that region, green in colour, and holding conch shells filled with sweetly-perfumed water. All these goddesses are extremely beautiful, and assembled in great numbers in their respective places. (33)

Uttering 'sun,' place a heap in the inner region of the east and visualize the sun within the innermost band of golden mountains. It shines brilliantly, with a hot light. (34)

Uttering 'moon,' place a heap in the inner region of the west and visualize the moon within the innermost band of golden mountains. It shines brilliantly, with a cold light. (35)

Uttering 'precious umbrellas,' place a heap in the inner region of the south and visualize that in the sky above the innermost band of mountains in the south are many ceremonial umbrellas. Their handles are made of gold, great jewels are set as knobs on the crests, and the cloth is that of the gods. (36)

Uttering 'banners of victory,' place a heap in the inner region of the north and visualize that in the sky above the innermost band of mountains in the north are many banners of victory, made of various kinds of cloth of the gods, with great jewels on their crests and handles of gold. (37)

Finally, pour a large handful of grains over the entire mandala, saying: 'This most perfect offering etc.' Also at this point during the process of offering the mandala, you should visualize as follows: the thirteen main places (that is, Mount Sumeru, the four major continents and the eight sub-continents) and the entire sky above them are filled with the eight auspicious articles (that is, precious parasol, golden fish, vase, lotus, white conch shell, magnificent knot, banner of victory and golden wheel), the eight auspicious materials (that is, the mirror, vermilion dye, white conch shell, medicine extracted from an elephant's brain, durva grass, bilva fruit, yoghurt, and white mustard seeds), the seven lesser riches of an emperor (that is, sleeping couch, throne, cushion, sword, shoes, snake-skin and robe), and the five objects of sense-desires (such as a mirror, fruit, cloth, cymbals and scented water). In short, it should be filled with all the riches and requirements that gods and humans desire, being lovely and in no way incomplete.

The mandala described here comprises one of the worlds of the realms of the four places (that is, the four cardinal points containing the four major continents). Now, you should regard the mandala as containing the greater world-system: first, one thousand worlds like this, which lie within the outer ring of the iron mountains, bound by a greater ring of iron mountains, comprise the system known as the 'first thousand.' The second thousand: a thousand complete one-thousand world systems, bounded by another iron mountain ring, make the system known as the 'second thousand.' The third thousand: a thousand of these second thousand systems, bounded within another wall, make up the system called the 'third thousand.' Visualize that from the greater mandala of the 'third thousand,' one hundred rays of light issue forth, each terminating in a 'great lotus' of precious substances as large as the third thousand itself. Each of these lotuses bear another third thousand system – all of them radiating light in one hundred beams, which also terminate in a 'third thousand bearing lotuses.' The process is repeated until the whole of space is filled with these mandalas. Each is clear, bright and distinct from the others.

If, during this offering, you give without losing the one-pointed condition of clear perception of the object of meditation, there will not be the slightest difference or deviation from the true offering, and as a result of this the two accumulations will soon be fully accomplished. (This means that there is no difference between the physical offering of a world and the meditation on offering a created world, provided the full one-pointed perception and concentration of the meditation object is maintained.) For this reason it is very important to preserve an undistracted mind, for if the mind is disturbed one will not be able to succeed in fulfilling the two accumulations, but only in the placing of many grains upon the mandala base.

This completes the teaching on the thirty-seven heap mandala offering, which should be offered several times each day. However, for the preliminary foundation practice, if you cannot offer this many times then you should perform one of the following offerings, such as the seven heap mandala together with counting.

Also, you should note that you must replace the grains every day, and it is good to add additional grains frequently. When changing the grains, the old materials should be taken outside and disposed of in a clean place, such as a hillside.

The seven heap mandala offering

> OM VAJRA BHUMI AH HUM
> The universe is wholly pure, of great power, with earth of gold.
> OM VAJRA REKHE AH HUM

The outermost limit of the universe is surrounded with an iron fence, and in the centre is the letter HUM. Here is the King of Mountains, Mount Sumeru, the eastern continent of Purvavideha, the southern continent of Jambudvipa, the western continent of Aparagodaniya, the northern continent of Uttarakuru, the sun and the moon. This most perfect offering of the wealth of gods and humans, to the greatly kind root guru and the lineage gurus who are glorious and holy, to the deities in the mandalas of the tutelary deities, to the Buddhas and bodhisattvas, to the protectors who guard the holy Dharma, and to the powerful gods of wealth, I offer. Through compassion, please accept it for the sake of living beings; having accepted it, please bestow your blessings.

In order to make the seven heap mandala offering, you should follow exactly the instructions given for the thirty-seven heap mandala offering from the beginning OM VAJRA BHUMI, etc. together with drawing the lines of the square and circle, etc., up to placing the grains in the centre while uttering the letter HUM. Then place heaps on the mandala for Mount Sumeru and the four continents, following the same procedure as in the long offering. Place a heap in the east saying 'sun' and visualizing the sun on the inner square band of golden mountains around Mount Sumeru, as in the longer mandala. Then place a heap in the west, while saying 'moon' and visualizing the moon on the inner square band of golden mountains. Then pour a handful of grain over the whole mandala, reciting, 'This most perfect offering, etc.'

The seven heap mandala offering by Sakya Pandita Kunga Gyaltsen

Here is a pure spiritual realm with Sumeru, King of Mountains, in the centre being adorned by the four continents and the five sense-desire objects, and traversed by a sun and moon. Also there is the wealth of gods and humans, whatever be desired, the seven precious articles of royalty, the wish-fulfilling cow, the wish-granting tree, uncultivated crops, gold and silver, and an inconceivable store of good grains, all wealth of the finest articles. Offering this to the guru and Buddhas, may I obtain the stage of a fully enlightened one.

The shortest mandala offering of seven heaps

This has a base of earth upon which scented water is applied and flowers are strewn and which is adorned by Mount Sumeru, the four continents, sun and moon; I imagine that this is offered to the realm of the Buddhas in order that all beings may be placed in a pure realm.

To conclude each session, you should recite the following mantra once:

OM GURU BUDDHA BODHISATTVA SAPARIWARA RAT-NA MANDALA PUJA MEGHA SAMUDRA SPHARANA SAMAYE HUM.

If you wish you may also recite the following prayer:

One's own offering ingredients are an ocean of pure realms adorned by a cloud of various offerings equal to the atoms of an ocean from which ornamental light rays issue in the ten directions, and at the tips of the rays are pure realms equal in number to the atoms of an ocean. At the end of each ray is a jewel-lotus which gives light from which the essence of the realms are produced. In these are the excellent sense-desire objects of gods and humans from which arises whatever one wishes abiding in the millions. Just like the miraculous offerings of Samantabhadra is this cloud of offering which is created by one's virtuous mind; this offering fills space just as the dharmadhatu pervades all; this offering remains so long as sentient beings and the dharmadhatu remain; I always offer to you. May you, the holy ones, who possess the eye of omniscience and who are most worthy of receiving offerings, through compassion for me, partake of these, my offerings; having accepted these, may you bless me.

4　The basic Vajrasattva meditation

In order to do this practice, you need the blessing and empowerment of a guru. Without this blessing the practice will be less powerful and beneficial.

First, the prayer of refuge and creation of the enlightenment thought.

> In the guru, Buddha, Dharma and the Sangha I take refuge until enlightenment is attained; by the merit of giving and other perfections, may I attain Buddhahood for the sake of all sentient beings. [Recite three times.]

In an instant, on the top of your head appears a lotus and moon-disc, upon which is seated the blessed one, Vajrasattva, whose body is white, with one face and two hands. In his right hand he holds a vajra to his heart and in his left a bell that rests in his lap and the cup of which points up to the left hip. Decorated with the six ornaments of bone, he wears precious robes of silk and he sits with his feet crossed in the vajra position. He bears the master of his race, the same in appearance as himself, on his head as a crown.

In the heart of Vajrasattva, on a moon–disc, is a white HUM. Rays of light issue forth from this, invoking the essence of mind of all Tathagatas which, in the form of the nectar of transcendental knowledge, is absorbed into the HUM.

Pray as follows:

O blessed one, cleanse and purify, I pray, all the accumulations of sins and obscurations, faults, failings and impurities which I and all sentient beings have collected throughout beginingless samsara.

Nectar falls from the HUM, filling the body of Vajrasattva. It descends from the entire body of Vajrasattva and, entering through the top of your head, drives out all illness, evil spirits, sins and obscurations, through the two lower passages as faeces and urine and through the two soles of the feet as smoky liquid or as pus and blood. The empty body is completely filled with nectar.

While maintaining this visualization of purification, recite the hundred-syllable mantra of Vajrasattva at least twenty-one times, or as many times as possible.

OM VAJRASATTVA SAMAYA MANUPALAYA VAJRASATT-
VA TVENOPATISHTA DRIDHO ME BHAVA SUTOSHYO ME
BHAVA SUPOKHOYO ME BHAVA ANURAKTO ME BHAVA
SARVASIDDHIM ME PRAYACCHA SARVAKARMASUCA
ME CITTAM SHREYAH KURU HUM HA HA HA HA HOH
BHAGAVAN SARVATATHAGATA VAJRA MA ME MUNCA
VAJRABHAVA MAHASAMAYASATTVA AH

Recite the following:
I, deluded by ignorance, have broken and spoiled the vows, guru and protector, be my refuge. To the highest Vajradhara, possessed of the essence of great compassion, the chief of beings, I go for refuge. I confess all my transgressions of the root and the branch vows of body, speech and mind. Cleanse and purify, I pray, all the accumulations of sins, obscurations, faults, failings and impurities.

Vajrasattva is pleased by your request, and responds:

O child of noble family, through your great faith this purification is effective; all of your impurities are cleansed and your vows are restored and renewed.

Vajrasattva then dissolves into light, which is absorbed into you through the top of your head, and your body becomes like a rainbow.

Dedication of merit:

> By this virtue may I attain the stage of Vajrasattva and quickly place upon his stage all beings without exception.

Notes on the meditation

At the time of the recitation of the hundred-syllable mantra these three visualizations should be concentrated upon for an equal length of time, so if you recite the mantra twenty-one times, then the first visualization should be performed during the recitation of the mantra seven times, the second visualization for the next seven times and the third visualization for the final seven recitations − if you recite the mantra three hundred times, the three visualizations should be maintained during each hundred recitations.

The three visualizations are as follows. First, in order to purify illnesses and disease; you should visualize the nectar that descends from Vajrasattva and enters into yourself as being of many colours. This nectar purifies all your illnesses and diseases, which are emitted from your body through the two lower passages, in the form of faeces and urine and through the soles of both feet, in the form of blood, pus and evil-smelling liquid.

Second, in order to purify yourself of evil spirits, demons and obstacles; the nectar descends from Vajrasattva in the form of copper-coloured liquid in which are many small Hayagrivas and Vajrapanis (wrathful deities). As the nectar fills your body, all the evil spirits depart through the two lower passages and the soles of your feet in the form of snakes, scorpions, spiders and other small unpleasant creatures.

Third, in order to purify sins and defilements, again, nectar descends from Vajrasattva in the form of white liquid. If fills your entire body and overflows at the top of your head and then flows down, covering your entire body. Visualizing that all sins, evil deeds and defilements leave your body through the two lower passages and soles of your feet in the form of dark, smoke-coloured liquid, imagine that the inside of your body is filled with pure nectar and the outside is covered with the same – thus, all inner and outer sins and defilements are purified.

In order to produce the right results from this meditation, it is necessary to bring to mind the four powers: shrine power, regret power, resolve power, and rejuvenating power. These four powers should always be kept in mind, and especially at the time of confession, which occurs in this meditation just after the conclusion of the recitation of the mantra.

1. *Shrine power.* This is the power of faith in the shrine to which you take refuge, confess sins, etc. In this meditation the shrine is the blessed one, Vajrasattva, who sits upon your head. Here Vajrasattva is the essence of the Triple Gem, and in him we place our faith and take refuge.

2. *Regret power.* This is the power of regret for all the bad actions of body, speech and mind that you have performed since beginningless samsara. You regret having done all these bad actions just as a person, having swallowed poison, has great regret.

3. *Resolve power.* This is the power of resolution never to perform non-virtuous actions of body, speech and mind again in the future. You resolve never again to do bad actions, even at the cost of your own life, and to diligently perform virtuous deeds for the benefits of yourself and all other sentient beings.

4. *Rejuvenating power.* This is the power of conviction in the effectiveness of this purification – that is, you have no doubt that all bad deeds, impurities, evil spirits and the like have been purified by this meditation. Having performed this meditation in the proper manner, you are certain beyond all doubt that all impurities have been washed away.

You should perform this meditation and recite the mantras one hundred thousand times, or until such time as the signs of purification arise. The signs of purification are that one becomes relaxed and peaceful in daily life; one is keen to perform virtuous deeds; one dreams of taking baths, flying in the sky, seeing dirty things or creatures leave one's body, drinking milk or curd, and so on.

This practice is one of the foundations for higher attainments without it you will not gain the realizations, no matter what profound teachings or initiations you receive. If you desire a good crop, you must first sow the seeds properly. Likewise, without the seed of proper purification, the crop of enlightenment will not grow.

5 Guru-yoga

In order to receive blessings, we perform guru-yoga. Guru-yoga is the essence of the Vajrayana path. For the superior person guru-yoga is the actual path to enlightenment; for the middling person it is the method of keeping the vows; for the inferior person it is the preliminary practice (by which he can later enter into the main path); and for the most inferior person it is the shrine for confessing broken vows.

Begin the practice by taking refuge and developing bodhicitta as explained, then visualize and recite the guru-yoga in the following way:

> On top of my head is a lion throne, sun and moon disc, upon which is my root guru, the all pervasive master Vajradhara, his body blue in colour with vajra and bell crossed at the heart. Adorned with ornaments of jewels and bones he wears waving silk garments, taking the sambogakaya form. From his heart light rays stream forth invoking the ten directions' gurus, deities, Buddhas, bodhisattvas, dharmapalas and wealth deities. They are non-dually absorbed into the guru who becomes the nature of all refuges.

Then recite the following verses of praise to the guru:

> Glorious, precious root guru seated on the lotus throne on the top of my head, having been accepted through your great kindness, please bestow the

attainments of body, voice and mind. I bow to the diamond-like feet of the preceptor whose body is like a jewel and by whose kindness the great bliss itself arises in a single moment. The guru is Buddha, the guru is Dharma, and likewise the guru is Sangha. The activities of all three are the guru, to the gurus I prostrate.

Having offered whatever praises to the guru that you know, recite the prayer to the root and lineage gurus such as the following lineage prayer of the Lam Dre Tshok Shay teaching of the Sakya tradition according to the lineage of His Holiness Sakya Trizin.

I pray to the four omniscient lamas who increased the harvest of the four emancipated bodies through having caused the incessant rain of the four very virtuous consecrations to fall upon the ground of the four very pure mandalas. I pray to the all-pervading one Vajradhara, Nairatmya, the lord of power, Mahasiddha Krishnapa, Damarupa, Avadhutipa and to Gayadhara. I pray to the great guru Drogmi, Seton Kunrig, Zangton Chobar, the auspicious Sakyapa, the reverend brothers Sonam Tsemo and Dagpa Gyaltsen, the learned lord of Dharma Sakya Pandita Kunga Gyaltsen and to Chogyal Phagpa. I pray to Konchog Pal, the lord of Dharma Sonam Pal, Sonam Gyaltsen, Palden Tsultim, Buddhashri, the great Ngorpa Vajradhara and to Sempa Chenpo. I pray to Kunga Wangchuk, the all-knowing Sonam Senge, Konchog Pel, Sangay Rinchen. I pray to Konchok Gyatso, Sonam Wangpo, Dagpa Lodro, Sangay Gyaltsen, Kunga Sonam, Sonam Wangchuk, and to Kunga Tashi. I pray to Sonam Rinchen, Sachen Kunlo, Kunga Tashi, Pema Dudul, Kunga Gyaltsen, Tashi Rinchen, and to Kunga Nyingpo. I pray to the real Vajradhara Karma Ratna, to the master of all races,

Zhenphen Nyingpo, to the lord of the cakra, Jampal Zangpo, and to all the glorious gurus. By the blessings of this prayer, renunciation and the two bodhicittas will rise within my heart. Having become enthusiastic through hearing of the qualities of the result bless me to enter into the path of the great secret.

Then recite the following one-verse prayer counting the number of recitations up to at least one hundred thousand.

To the precious guru, the collection of all places of refuge, the greatly kind master of Dharma, I pray: matchless, benevolent one, look upon me with compassion and bless me always in this life, the next and the intermediate state.

Without being distracted by other thoughts reflect on the knowledge that the guru is the essence of all objects of refuge. There is no one else who can bestow the common and excellent attainments. Having produced deep and strong devotion, continue to pray and meditate in this way.

At the end of the session recite and visualize the following:

The holy guru, being very pleased, dissolves into light and is absorbed into the top of my head. My three doors and the guru's three secrets (his body, voice and mind) become non-differentiated. The four obscurations (of body, voice, mind and all three together) are purified, the four consecrations attained and seeds of the four bodies planted within my mind continuum.

Now relax the mind and cut conceptual thoughts. Meditate on the understanding of the mind: that its nature is nothing whatsoever — the dharmakaya, that its shade is not stopped anywhere — the sambhogakaya, great devotion continues to be active — the nirmanakaya, that it is devoid of meditation and meditator — the svabavikakaya. If thoughts arise while meditating remember the qualities of the guru and produce a strong desire to follow his activities.

Seal the session with a dedication and prayers, such as:

> In every birth, never being apart from the real guru and through thoroughly accomplishing the attainment of the magnificent Dharma and the qualities of the stages and path, may I quickly attain the stage of Vajradhara.

This is the practice of guru-yoga as it is explained in the common teachings only. Important points of the uncommon practice should be learned from the commentaries and from the mouth of the guru himself.

Appendices

1 A short history of the Sakya tradition

The prophecy of Palden Atisha

When the Indian Mahapandit, Palden Atisha, left behind him the snow-covered mountains on the Tibetan border, he crossed the southernmost regions of Tsangtsos and moved northward through the province on his way to Tholing. He passed the elephant-shaped mountain called Ponpori, a landmark for the part of the country later known as Sakya. Resting on the bank of the river which flows along at the foot of the mountain, he let his gaze wander over the mountain scenery before him.

On the mountain's dark slope, a large, mirror-like patch of white earth was visible. Near it, two black wild yaks were grazing. On seeing them, Palden Atisha turned to the disciples accompanying him and made the prediction that in the future two emanations of Mahakala, the protector of the holy Buddhadarma, would appear in that place.

The guru then made prostrations in the direction of the white disc, on the circumference of which he saw seven shining images of the letter DHI, the mantric symbol of the bodhisattva Manjushri. Shining radiantly there, too, were the letters HRIH and HUNG, the symbolic signs of Avalokitesvara and Vajrapani. The vision of these letters, so Palden Atisha explained, signified that seven emanations of Manjushri and one each of Avalokitesvara and Vajrapani would also appear for the benefit of all beings. Through many centuries of Tibetan history indications were found that led to the fulfilment of this prophecy.

The Sakya Khon dynasty

The story goes that a long time ago three brothers of the celestial race called Lha-rig descended from the Abhasvara heaven and settled on the peak of a salt-crystal mountain in Tibet. Although the two elder brothers, Ciring and Yuring, soon returned to celestial regions, the youngest, Yuse, remained on earth, together with his family. His great-grandson, Yapang Kye, married Ya-drug Silima, who gave birth to a boy. This boy was called Khonbar Kye. With him began the earthly lineage which was later known as the Khon dynasty. References to these events were found in the Tibetan history book, *Saskya Gpun Rabs Chen Mo*.

The descendants of this lineage were held in great esteem. They were well known for their generosity, their virtue and their authority. In course of time, one branch of the Khon family reached the Sakya valley, south of the rivers Tsangpo and Rhe. They settled there and for thirteen generations practised the Buddhist teachings of the Nyingmapa school which was brought from India and taught by Padmasambhava. However, in the fourteenth hierarchy headed by Sherab Tshultim, they parted from this religious tradition. The reason for this was said to be Sherab Tshultim's dismay at the frequent public display of tantric symbols and their concealed meaning which, so he thought, would be damaging to other yogis. He therefore decided that from then onwards only new tantras from India should be taught.

For this reason he sent his younger brother, Konchog Gyalpo, to Mugulung in order to study with the well-known translator Drogmi Lotsava who was a contemporary of Palden Atisha's. Drogmi Lotsava was a student of the saint Gayadhara and possessed extensive knowledge of the tantras. He became one of the foremost teachers of his time. It was through him, as well as through other gurus, that Konchog Gyalpo acquired comprehensive knowledge of these new Indian tantric methods after many years of devoted study and practice. When he was forty years of age, he searched for a place to build a monastery. He chose an area beneath the large white spot on Ponpori mountain and the monastery was named Sakya (white earth), after the region in which it was built.

In the year 1092, Konchog Gyalpo's wife gave birth to a boy named Sachen Kunga Nyingpo. Already, from early childhood onwards, and way ahead of his age, this boy showed signs of great wisdom and intellectual ability, especially with regard to religious teachings, which he received from his father. At the age of eleven, he practised Arapacana Manjushri's sadhana under the guidance of Bari Lotsava. After meditating on this subject for six months, Arya Manjushri appeared and gave him his teaching, together with the essence of the Zenpa Zidel doctrine, the parting from the four attachments. This doctrine (snin-po) originated with the Adi-Buddha, who is the source of all Dharmas.

After Sachen Kunga Nyingpo had absorbed all the preachings of Arya Manjushri, he handed them down to his two sons, Sonam Tsemo and Dagpa Gyaltsen. The latter in turn, then passed them on to Sakya Pandita who transferred these teachings to Chogyal Phagpa.

Since then, these teachings in their original version have been handed down to twenty-seven successive Sakya hierarchs. The current Sakya Trizen, His Holiness Ngawang Kunga, resides at the present time, at the Sakya Centre in Dehra Dun, India.

The five Sakyapas mentioned above bear witness to the fulfilment of Palden Atisha's prophecy. Kunga Nyingpo's four sons, together with Sakya Pandita, Zangtsha Sonam Gyaltsen and Chogyal Phagpa were recognized during the course of their lives, as the seven emanations of Manjushri. Dogon Changa Dorje was considered to be an emanation of Vajrapani, owing to his superhuman powers.

The wild yaks represent the two wrathful deities who were chosen by Sachen Kunga Nyingpo to protect the Sakya doctrine. Sachen himself was a reincarnation of Avalokitesvara, the bodhisattva of all-embracing compassion.

After this, lamas appeared in succession as emanations of Manjushri and, as a result, many great bodhisattvas, the praised protectors of all beings, appeared in Sakya, one after the other. They secured the new tantras from India and integrated them into the religious life of Tibet by means of the Sakya teaching methods. They taught the Lam Dre teaching (the path and its fruits) in order to show the way to complete enlightenment and they carried these teachings as far as China and Mongolia.

2 *An autobiography of the author*

OM SVASTI! I BOW TO MANJUSHRI!

The holy land of Sakya, where I was reborn, is the sacred place in Tibet which is similar to Bodhgaya in India. The Indian pandit Atisa, travelling for the first time to Tibet, as mentioned in the last section, had a vision in Sakya of seven letter DHIH's, one letter HRIH, and one letter HUNG, which symbolized that seven emanations of Manjushri, one emanation of Avalokitesvara and one emanation of Vajrapani would come to the holy land of Sakya, to work for the sake of living beings. Pandit Atisa also saw two yaks grazing on the side of the Sakya mountain called Ponpori; these two yaks signified that two manifestations of Mahakala would be working there for the cause of Dharma.

Thus I was born in Sakya, the holy land of emanations, to the Amipa family, an old family from the town of Sakya. Tibetan families are rather large; they include aunts and uncles, grandparents and other relatives. In my family, there were seven people.

My father, Dorje Amipa, was a government official. Patience was his chief characteristic and his religious practices enabled him to help the sick very effectively. He meditated intensely on Avalokitesvara, and his yidam was Hevajra. Every morning before going to work, he fulfilled many offerings to the protectors of the Dharma and to Paldan Lhamo, the special dharmapala (personal protector) of our family, and also performed sadhanas. Unfortunately, he did not live very long and died when I was only seven years old.

My mother, Tashi Wangmo, came from a farming family in the village of Yalung, close to the town of Sakya. She had a deep faith in the Dharma; her Dharma practice consisted of Avalokitesvara in his six-armed form, and of the Prayer to the Twenty-one Green Taras, which she recited several times a day. She also believed strongly in Padmasambhava. My mother was a very mild and sensitive woman; often, when she heard of someone in great distress, she would cry. It was her greatest wish that our family and neighbours should live in a close, united community.

My uncle was a doctor; by tradition in our family, one male descendant of each generation would choose this profession. The study of Tibetan medicine consists of much more than just learning texts. Our family owned large statues of the eight Medicine Buddhas, and, every year, my uncle and other lamas spent many weeks praying to these Medicine Buddhas while the remedies were being prepared, to be distributed afterwards. These remedies consisted of plants which my uncle collected in the mountains three times a year, when they were in full bloom, and of different kinds of precious stones. Some of the remedies were imported from India at great expense. The prepared remedies were kept in decorated wooden trunks in a special room in our house; each remedy was preserved in a little leather bag with the name of the medicine engraved on a silver plaquette. Sometimes patients came to our house and sometimes my uncle went to visit them in their villages.

My grandfather also lived in our house; I cannot remember him very well. I only know that he was very pious, always reciting the mantra OM MANI PADME HUNG.

I had one brother and two sisters. One of my sisters died early. My elder brother Shedhub Tendzin entered the Sakya monastery Lhakhang Chenmo when he was eight years old. He studied religious philosophy and Mahayana; at the age of thirty-three, he reached the grade of Geshe Rabjampa and taught religious philosphy in the monastery.

My sister Sodhön was very kind to me. After my brother

had been accepted into the monastery we played together often. Sometimes she took me to town. During the summer, we played in the pond in our garden. We loved building little houses out of the earth. Sometimes we played with other children using coloured pebbles for toys and sometimes we all did the cooking – our dishes weren't very clean! During all the winter we used to play at the riverside close by, when it was frozen over.

My uncle Hridsin, who was twenty years older than me, lived in the neighbourhood. Like my father, he was a government official and he was married with four children. Today, two of his daughters live in Mysore, South India, and one daughter in Darjeeling.

Our family owned a lot of land. In spring and autumn, we usually engaged farm-hands, who lived in our house for the season. As well as housekeeping, my mother helped to sow, to water and to harvest, supervising the farm lands. We also had many horses, donkeys and cows. The horses were mainly used for journeys, and the donkeys for carrying loads. When a calf was born, my mother made butter from the first milk of the cow, and put it in the big, golden butterlamp of the main temple of the monastery of Thubten Lhakhang Chenmo. We also prepared buttercheese and offered this to my teachers, the lamas, and we ate it ourselves too.

Generally, our food consisted of tsampa, made of barley or beans, white bread, cheese, butter, meat, some rice, and vegetables of the season. Sometimes we got sugar and other delicacies from India. We had two kinds of tea: a dark one from India, which we drank with sugar, and one from Eastern Tibet, which we used for butter-tea. Although some Tibetans drink wine and beer, no one in our family liked alcohol.

Every family has a special dharmapala: ours was Palden Lhamo. On the roof of our house there was a *tharpung*, a kind of reliquary, containing several pictures of the protectress. We made many offerings to the goddess each day and once a month we said a special prayer. At new year, the celebrations were always performed with great splendour; everybody got presents and wore new clothes; new banners were raised, and *kapasa* (a ceremonial cake) was offered. The festivities lasted for more than three days. Then, from the tenth to the twenty-fifth day of the first month, we celebrated, with many offerings and butterlamps, the anniversary of the twelve great deeds of Buddha Shakyamuni.

I was born in 1931. My mother told me that she was full of joy at the moment of my birth, and that she felt no pain. When I was still very young, she asked a lama about me; he told her that I should lead a very pure life. When I was a small boy, I gave her little trouble although my brother Shedhub had a lot of problems. When I was seven years, my family sent me to the monastery to become a monk. My ordination was chosen to be on the full-moon day of the seventh Tibetan month, because it was a very auspicious day astrologically − from the point of view of the planets as well as from my own horoscope. I was very happy that day. My mother had always wanted me to enter the monastery; and at my ordination she was delighted that I would spend my whole life as a monk for the Buddhadharma.

At my ordination my family brought many offerings − gifts for the temple and tea for the monks. My abbot was the venerable Jampal Tangpo and the ceremony took place in the room containing the throne of the first Tibetan Dharma King, Chogyal Phagpa, in Thubten Lhakhang Ladhang. At that time I received the name Sherab Gyaltsen, meaning wisdom (prajna) banner of religion.

The ritual of the monk's ordination lasted an hour. First my hair was completely shaved except for a small tuft on top of my head. Then, together with an exquisite white blossom, called *tsampakha*, this last tuft was cut too and offered to the Buddha. That day I took first the Upsaka vow and then the vow of a novice monk. During this ceremony, two things are changed: a religious name is substituted for one's own name and one's clothing is exchanged for a monk's robe. At the end of the ritual, the abbot recited a prayer to share merit, gave me a present and conferred his blessing in the form of a red cord.

After the ritual was over, my mother, my brother and I went to the temple to offer butterlamps and khatas (offering scarfs) to the Buddha. Then we went to visit the lama who was going to look after me in the monastery. We stayed for some hours, drank tea, and received special rice with fruit and other gifts, symbolizing good omens. After the ceremony my mother returned home. During the time that I was training as a monk I was not allowed to visit my family, except for vacations. Sometimes my mother came to see me in the monastery and brought me presents. At the beginning I was very homesick.

Traditionally in Tibet, the family of a novice chooses a monk to serve him as a protector. The novice lives with this protector in the monastery and is provided with food, clothing and everything he needs. The protector is not the guru of the novice, although he is generally also capable of giving some fundamental religious instruction. My protector taught me to write on a blackboard with a bamboo pencil and I had to memorize prayers in addition to my regular homework for the monastery school. Every morning he sent me to the temple for the morning prayer and to the monastery school.

During the first year I learnt to read and write; I learnt the Chö-Chö (*chos-mchod*) by heart, which is a collection of prayers to the Buddhas, bodhisattvas, gurus and others recited in our monastery. This book comprises about a hundred pages. I studied the Du-dha (*bsdus-grva*), which serves as a preparation for the study of the Pramana, and the Rig-lam (*rigs-lam*), the path of logic concerning the analysis of the form and path of knowledge. These studies took a year and a half. During this time, I also memorized the texts of the different rituals which were followed in the monastery, namely that of Vairocana, the White Tara, Usnisavijaya, the Medicine Buddhas and others. I also received private lessons on Sakya Pandita's *Wishing Treasure of Elegant*

Sayings, with commentary *(legs-bshad-'dod-dgu-'byung-bai-gter-mdsod).* All these studies comprise the Ka-zhi *(bka'-bzhi).*

My principal teacher, who gave me lessons on the Ka-zhi and gave me most of the other spiritual teachings during the first three years was venerable Khenpo Sanggya Rinchen. He was a geshe of a higher level and later on served for five years as head abbot of the Monastery of Sakya Thubten Lhakhang Chenmo. He had studied tantra and yoga and gave instructions on several different subjects to all the monks at the monastery. He has also been the guru of His Holiness Jigdhal Dagchen Rinpoche, the principal of the Sakya Phuntshog Palace; after his official period as abbot, he went with His Holiness to Kham, in Eastern Tibet.

At the university of Sakya Thubten Lhakhang Chenmo, one generally studies the complete teachings of the Buddha, which are essentially compiled into the six great books, as follows: (1) the Paramitas; (2) Pramana; (3) Vinaya; (4) Abhidharama; (5) Madhyamika: and (6) the three kinds of vows. After the preparatory study of the Du-dha, I studied the Pramana for five years. The texts I learnt included the *Tshad-ma-kun-btus* (Sanskrit, *Pramanasamuccaya)* of the Indian pandit Dinnaga, the *Tshad-masde-bdun* of his disciple Dhamakirti and the *Tshad-ma-rnam-'grel, ri-gter-gsal-byed* and the *Tshad-ma-sde-bdun* of Sakya Pandita. Each book has about sixty to eighty pages.

During my Pramana studies I received the initiation of the Buddha Ayutara, the Buddha of Long Life; from His Holiness Sakya Dagchen Ngawang Thutob Wangchug I received the initiation of the guru-yoga of Sakya Pandita, who is an emanation of the Buddha of wisdom, Manjushri. I practise this sadhana every day as it is extremely important for the development of wisdom.

Every winter and summer, during my Pramana studies, I used to visit two small monasteries, one for monks and the other for nuns, which were both a day's journey from the monastery. These two monasteries belonged to my main guru. My visits, usually lasting ten days were most enjoyable since the monks and nuns were very honest and respectful; I would in fact have preferred to stay there rather than return to the head monastery.

For two years I led morning prayers in the monastery. These prayers were usually taken from the Chö-Chö. On special days, such as new year or the birthday of the Buddha, I led the singing; on these days the monks wore special garments and they sat on long benches, and the Sakya government offered us tea and cakes. I had to memorize a great deal from the Chö-Chö, because different kinds of chants were performed on each special day. In summer, when the star Rig-yas appeared, we held a ceremony. On one occasion during this ceremony I sang the story of the meeting of Arya Asanga, and Buddha Maitreya entirely from memory. This solemn chant lasted two hours.

When I finished my five-year Pramana studies at the age of thirteen, I had reached the level of *bris-pa-rgan-pa*.

I then studied for five years the ten Paramitas — mainly the *Five Dharmas of Maitreya (byams-chos-sde-lnga)*:

1. *Mahayanasutralamkarakarika (theg-pa-chen-po-mdo-sde-rgyan)*
2. *Madhyanta-Vibhanga (dbus-dang-mtha'-rnam-par-'byed-pa)*
3. *Dharma-Dharmata-Vibhanga (cho-dang-chos-nyid-rnam-par-'byed-pa)*
4. *Mahayanottaratantra (theg-pa-chen-po-rgyud-bla-ma'i-bstan-bcos)*
5. *Abhisamayalamkara (mngon-par-rtogs-pa'i-rgyan)*

These were all received by Arya Asanga from the Buddha Maitreya. The commentaries have been written by Tibetan scholars such as Kunkhyen Gorampa Sonam Senge and others.

I also studied Santideva's *Spyod-'jug* (Sanskrit: *Bodhicaryavatara*), where the main subjects are the six Paramitas. I learnt the fundamental text by heart, which the teacher explained word by word, and I studied the commentaries of

Indian and Tibetan scholars, especially the commentary of Lopon Sonam Tsemo, one of the five early Sakyapa masters.

Every year, great festivities were held at the summer and winter solstices. During the summer festivities, when I was seventeen, I received the great teaching of Lam Dre, which was brought to Tibet by the holy Indian Mahasiddha Virupa. The explanations were divided in two parts: the *snag-gsum*, which contains fundamental Buddhist lessons, and the *rgyad-gsum*, which puts emphasis on the Tantric aspect; the study of each of these subjects took half a year. Then followed the initiations of the four classes of Tantra (*bya-bai-rgyud, spyod-pai-rgyud, rnal-byor-rgyud, rnal-byor-bla-na-med-pa'i-rgyud;* Sanskrit: *Kriyatantra, Caryatantra, Yogatantra, Anuttarayogatantra*) and initiations for all forms of all Buddhas and bodhisattvas; several initiations were necessary for each Buddha and bodhisattva. Some of the initiations were given to groups of twenty-one students.

During that year I also made various short retreats, which included introductory practices (*sngon-'gro*), silence meditation (*shi-gnas,* Sanskrit: *samatha*) and insight meditation which are the basis for further meditation.

When I was eighteen I passed the very important examination of Kacu (*bka'-bcu*), which opened the way to further studies to reach the grade of a Geshe Rabjampa. I prepared for this examination with the greatest diligence: I ate no meat and lived especially virtuously. All morning I sat over the commentaries and at night I recited the texts. I had memorized the texts so well that I could see whole lines and pages in front of me, even in the dark.

My family were also very keen that I should do well in this exam. The day before, they raised new prayer flags on the mountain near our house, and brought offerings and prayers to Green Tara.

The examination took place on the morning of the twenty-second day of the eleventh Tibetan month. The student was examined by his master and by the abbot, and the examination took place in the room of the Dharma

King, Chogyal Phagpa, in Lhakhan Lhadhang. After passing the exam, I was given a khata (scarf) according to the grade I had achieved. I felt deep peace within, even deeper than the feeling I had later on, when I reached the grade of a geshe; I was so happy that I had no recollection of going down the many steps which led from the monastery to my parents' house. My family waited for me and when they saw the khata, they were delighted as this meant that I had passed my exam. Afterwards, we celebrated the event for three days: my family, teachers, relatives and friends. They gave me khatas and presents. A month later I made a large offering to the community of the monastery, consisting of tea, bread and other things. Then I had some free time and I was able to sometimes take part in picnics during that summer.

After that I made a retreat for a month on a certain yidam. When I had finished the retreat, I was allowed to make the mandala of this yidam and to give initiations on the first two levels of tantra.

Before I had passed the Kacu exam, and up to the main studies of the tantras, I wore the yellow monk's hat, according to the vinaya. There were thirty-five stitches at the top of the hat, symbolizing the Confessional Buddhas; at the back were sixteen stiches in a row symbolizing the Sixteen Arhats. The hat was covered with stitches, which symbolize the thousand Buddhas of this kalpa. The hat had been made according to the level of my studies. The cloth was black, with a red top, that reached from the front to the back of the hat.

Each year the Sakya Dolma Palace and the Phuntshog Palace arranged a four-day festival in the main Sakya monastery, where the complete Kangyur text was read. The day after the readings, pujas for Mahakala and other gods were recited and during that time I led the cham (tantric dances) of the different dharmapalas.

Having reached the Kacu grade, I studied Abhidharma Buddhist metaphysics. One studies the origins of the universe the nature and the detailed explanation of the six realms, and the different realms of Buddha – in short, a quantitative analysis of the universe. The texts are: *The Complete Collection of the Abhidharma (mngon-pa-kun-btus)* and *the Treasure of Abhidharma (chos-mngon-pa'i-mdsod)* together with the commentaries of Panchen Ngawang Chodhag and Gorampa Sonam Senge, and also the Abhidharma of the Indian pandit Vasubhandu. This, together with additional studies of the Paramitas, is the preparation for the grade of geshe. For two years I studied the Abhidharma and received more teachings and initiations during that time. After that, I studied Madhyamika for two years. The main text I learnt was the Madhyamikavatara *(dbu-ma-'jug-pa)* of Nagarjuna, with the commentaries of Gorampa Sonam Senge and Panchen Ngawang Chodhag.

At the age of twenty, on the festival day of the Buddha's descent from Tusita, I received complete ordination as a monk. My abbot was the venerable Khenpo Manto and the ceremony took place in the presence of ten monks in Thubten Lhakhan Lhadhang. For a long time after this, I would not eat any meat and could not eat more than one meal a day. After my ordination I went on a pilgrimage to the three holy places, to meditate. The first place was the monastery of Utse, where the sword of Manjushri is kept. This precious holy sword can only be seen by special permission. According to your spiritual development, you can see different shapes in it.

For instance, you can see the forms of several Buddhas and bodhisattvas. There is also a holy statue of Manjushri. There are other holy images and books. I meditated there for a day.

Next day, I visited the monastery of Sakya Gorum, where there is a special underground temple to Mahakala, the protector of the Dharma. (In earlier times, the Sakya masters were able to speak directly with Mahakala.) In the upper part of the monastery is the Lama Lhakham (temple of the guru), in which is kept a holy statue of Sakya Pandita, made by Lama Tsangnag Phugpa, and which has been sanctified from far away by Sakya Pandita himself.

From there, I went for several days into a meditation cave in which Sachen Kunga Nyingpo received his teachings, known as *The Parting from the Four Attachments* (*zhen-pa-bzhi-bral*). After Madhyamika, I started on the three kinds of vows. The basic text was Sakya Pandita's book *The Three Vows* (*sdom-gsum*). As regards the pratimoksa vows, I studied the *Pratimoksa Sutra* (*sos-thar-pa'i-mdo*), as well as the commentaries of the Indian pandit Gunaprabha and of Agamamula (*mdo-rtsa-ba*), and the commentaries of the Tibetan scholar Kunkhyen Gorampa Sonam Senge. 'Pratimoksa' generally means the seven classes of ordination (male and female, laymen-students, novices, bhiksu, bhiksuni and gelobma) and other rules and instructions of the Buddha. After the pratimoksa, I studied the bodhisattva vows and an explanation of bodhicitta.

Then for three years I studied the tantric vow, which starts with Hevajra. I learnt the basic text by heart and read many commentaries. The more profound studies of tantra are undertaken after becoming a geshe. Following the study of the three vows, I was prepared for my examination for geshe. According to our tradition, my guru performed a *mo* (prophecy), to decide what should be done to avoid all obstacles. The answer was that I should do the ritual of the Sixteen Arhats, pray to Green Tara, recite the Sutra of the Essence Wisdom, and offer prayers to my guru. For this, I invited ten lamas to my house and recited these prayers for three days.

The first part of the geshe exam was held in the Manjushri Lhakan of the Utse monastery before the whole community. The exam lasted four days from nine o'clock in the morning to five o'clock in the afternoon. From there we went to the nearby Sakya Tshog, where every Sakya Trizin is crowned and where he takes his place on the throne of the Dharma King Chogyal Phagpa. Here we were examined for three days, from ten o'clock to four o'clock. When all this was over, I was given the title of a Geshe Rabjampa (master of the psycho-ethical philosophy); I gave offerings to all the assembled monks.

Shortly after this, I made a retreat for three months. I started at six o'clock every morning and meditated four times a day; during each sitting I made offerings to my yidam and to my guru, and did a special sadhana every fourth time at the end of the day. During this time I was completely isolated from the outside world — except for two servants. The retreat was most beneficial; I felt quite changed inside, with a great sense of peace and strong concentration, through the power of the blessing of my holy guru, the holy Buddhadharma and my yidam. At the end of the retreat, I made a large offering for three days called jin-sag. This is a fire-offering composed of different plants, seeds, butter, and so on. After this I made further large offerings, called tsog.

My daily meditation during this time consisted of *The Four Deep Meditations of the Sakyapa for Every Day* (Hevajra, Vajra Yogini, guru-yoga and the guru-yoga of Virupa) together with other sadhanas. After finishing the retreat, I studied *The Thirteen Golden Dharmas of Sakya* (*sa-skya-gser-chos-gsom*) and tantric teachings on the nadis. To practise tantra, you need a guru, a yidam and a god of wealth. Many practitioners of tantra have more than one yidam; in this case a yidam is considered to be a cig-du (*gcig-bsdus*) who owns all the qualities of all yidams and all subjects of refuge, all in one.

A guru is someone who has attained a high level of spiritual understanding and who is able to teach on all aspects of the Buddhadharma. The guru is the person who puts the seed of the four Buddha bodies (*sprul-sku, longs-sku, chos-sku, nog-bo-nyid-sku;* Sanskrit: *nirmanakaya, sambhogakaya, dharmakaya, svabhavikakaya* into the nature and spirit of the disciple; the guru is the one who represents Vajradhara for the disciple. This is the reason why there must be a strong relationship between guru and disciple; if there is not, the student will not be open to the power of the guru. The word guru is used only for those who convey tantric initiations to a disciple. Someone who teaches but does not give initiations is called master, or Lopon (*slob-spon*). From my root guru, His Holiness Sakya Dagchen Ngawang Thutob Wangchug, I received tantric initiations of many yidams during the course of a year: different forms and colours of Manjushri and Mahakala, Green Tara and White Tara, dakinis, (female emanations of the Buddha) Hevajra, Kalacakra, Vajra Yogini, Vajrakila and others.

In the guru lineage of the Sakyas there are emanations of Avalokitesvara, Manjushri and Vajrapani. My guru, His Holiness the fifth Sakya Trizin, was an emanation of Manjushri, and I visualized his true nature as Buddha Vajradhara. His Holiness was most generous to the people of Sakya and especially to those in the monastery. With great compassion, he enlarged the existing classes and schools in the Sakya monastery, for the benefit of all the inhabitants. Spiritually, he was very powerful: he had the ability to see the future and to accomplish miracles. Once he created a well that miraculously bubbled up in a Sakya village and survived severe drought. Another time, when workers came to renovate part of the Sakya monastery and could not find the right kind of stone for the columns, His Holiness prayed hard to the Dharma protector Mahakala, who then caused the earth to open up close to the monastery and reveal large blocks of stone − enough to renovate the whole monastery. My guru was also a servant of the dakini Sungma, and he could actually see her and talk to her. These were his outer qualities, visible to anyone; his inner nature was beyond all perception.

After I had reached the grade of geshe, I started to give extensive lectures myself. There were some Sakya monasteries some distance away, but I did not want to go there very much; I preferred to stay in the main monastery, teaching the monks and sometimes laymen who lived in the vicinity.

Two years after I became a geshe, my mother died. Her

death made me very sad. She had only been sick a few days, and when she knew that she was going to die, she gave exact instructions on what to do after her death. According to Tibetan tradition, the body is burnt three to seven days after death. The lamas performed religious ceremonies, like the ritual Vairocana and the *Bardo Thödol* was read for seven weeks after her death. During this time a number of lamas and monks came to our house, bringing many offerings. My mother's body was burnt, and I repeated the Vairocana mantra a million times over the ashes, together with other lamas: we then made dust from the ashes and formed little stupas, repeating the same mantra over and over again.

An astrologer drew a horoscope of the moment of my mother's death. This is done in order to know the tendencies of the dead person for the next life in a certain realm, and to find out which statues, thangkas and other things should be set up in order to warrant a human rebirth. We built statues of Buddha Shakyamuni and Vajrasattva for my mother.

In 1956, three years before the Chinese invaded Lhasa, they ordered a meeting of delegates from all the monasteries. The Sakya government sent me, and when the Chinese took me from Shigatse to Lhasa it was my first ride in a car. In Lhasa I stayed in a Sakya house, near Ramoche. The other lamas and geshes and I had between two and four meetings a week with the Chinese, for approximately three months. Apart from these encounters, I was very happy to see the image of Jhowo and Buddha Shakyamuni, and to say prayers and give offerings in the sacred temple of Lhasa; I was able to visit other temples in Lhasa, and even the Potala Palace of His Holiness the Dalai Lama. After three months, I told the Chinese that I did not want to stay any longer and I returned to Sakya. On my return, the Sakya government informed me of the result of the meeting. And so I stayed in Sakya and continued to give lessons to my students there.

In 1954, the Chinese came to Sakya for the first time, but since there were only a few of them life went on as usual. In

1959, after the conflicts in Lhasa, His Holiness Sakya Trizin left Tibet and went to India. The situation in Sakya became very difficult the following year. Six months after His Holiness moved to India the Chinese gathered all the lamas to an inquiry and then took them to a 'school,' as they called it, though in reality it was a prison. I would have had to go there too, if I had not been sick. The Chinese sent one of their doctors to test whether I was really ill. I did not like being treated by a Chinese doctor very much, although I had the feeling that this one sincerely tried to help people. He gave me several injections and in the course of a week I felt a lot better. I then prayed for three days and performed a mo, to decide whether I should stay in Sakya or try to go to India. The answer was that I should leave, and I began to make plans for my departure; this happened in the eleventh Tibetan month, 1959.

Together with a geshe and one of my students, I departed. We had four horses and very little luggage; since I was still a little weak, I went on horseback part of the way. The journey from Sakya to India generally takes two weeks, but since we did not know the way, it took us three weeks. We were lucky in meeting a man on the way who guided us to Gangtok, Sikkim.

When our group arrived at the border of Sikkim, the Indian government was kind enough to send us a car, which took us to Kalimpong. Three of our horses did not last to the end of the journey and I gave the last one to a person in Sikkim for a hundred rupees. On the road to Gangtok I met countless refugees who had fled before me and we were all very happy to see each other again.

Kalimpong seemed to us like a dream, after our long and difficult journey. We stayed at the house of some Tibetan friends there, recovered and performed prayer rituals for our host family. I also got an Indian passport there.

I then entered the Sakya guru monastery of Darjeeling, where there are approximately fifty monks. It was founded by Sakya Trizin with the help of many donations. Here I stayed for two years and I was very happy because the tradition was the same as at home in Tibet.

In India there was an English nun, Mrs Freda Bedi, who was very interested in helping lamas. First, she consulted His Holiness the Dalai Lama, then the Tibetan government, and later on the heads of the Sakya, Gelug, Kagyu and Nyingma schools. With their consent, and with the help of numerous references from Europe and America, she founded schools for all four traditions of Tibetan Buddhism, for the young lama tulkus. His Holiness Sakya Trizin chose four lama tulkus and me as representatives of the Sakya to study there.

In the school we studied Buddhist religion, English, Hindi, Punjabi and geography and each year we had different teachers from England, America and Germany. The school building was excellent and we were given food there, which also came from abroad, as did our clothing. We had classes in spring, summer and autumn and in winter there was a break. During these vacations I used to visit Bodhgaya, Sarnath and other holy places. Sometimes I travelled to the Sakya Centre in Rajpur, where I received many teachings on Vajra Yogini by His Holiness Sakya Trizin.

On another occasion, I went to see my niece in South Mysore; the journey took five days and nights. Of course we were delighted to see each other again, but her living conditions were difficult. She had her own house, but she also had three children and not very much land: life was quite hard. I stayed at her place for two months. Three years later, I was told that her situation had improved but I could not go and see her as it was too far away.

One day, when I was living in Dalhousie, I received a letter from Dharamsala, saying that I should go to the Tibetan Institute in Switzerland. I wrote back, asking who had decided this. The Tibetan government said that many Tibetan refugees were living in Switerland, and that the religious needs of the Tibetans there should be met to preserve their religion and culture and to create links be-

tween Tibetans and those Europeans who were interested in
Dharma. His Holiness the Dalai Lama and the Tibetan
government had chosen me and four other lamas to live in
this institute. I wrote to His Holiness Sakya Trizin, asking
for his opinion, and he approved of the project.

It took about three months to get the exit permit from the
Indian government, and in the meantime I travelled to Rajpur to say goodbye to His Holiness Sakya Trizin; I received his blessing, and some special instructions about the
Thirteen Golden Dharmas.

On 23 June 1967 I left Dalhousie for the palace of His
Holiness the Dalai Lama in Dharamsala. There the other
lamas and I met His Holiness twice. During the first visit,
His Holiness gave us some good advice; at the second
meeting, he gave us the holy book of the *Prajnaparamita*, a
picture of himself for the monastery, and a signed picture
for each of us. When we left, His Holiness gave us his
blessing. From there we went to Patankot by car, and to
New Delhi by train, where we stayed for a few days for
medical examinations and to prepare documents for the
journey at the Tibetan embassy. On 12 July 1967, we went
by train from New Delhi to Bombay and then by air to
Zurich. At the airport, we were welcomed by Mr Thubten
Phala, Mr Kuhn, Professor Lindegger, deputies from the
Red Cross, journalists and a number of other people. (Mr
Thubten is the personal representative of His Holiness the
Dalai Lama.) We had tea at the airport and then went on to
Rikon.

The first year, before the Institute was finished, we lived
in a house in the village. Everything was so different for us,
especially in wintertime. Because we did not have watches,
we never knew what time it was. We were all very homesick. That first year was extremely difficult as we could not
understand people very well, although we had German lessons. But sometimes Tibetan people came to see us, or we
went to visit them, and this gave us great pleasure. During
these visits. I gave some religious teachings to the Tibetan

children and performed prayer rituals for their families. Some months after my arrival in Switzerland, I was invited by Mr Phala to go to Geneva. He showed me the town, the lake and the United Nations building. I was especially impressed by the UN conference halls and the headphones for simultaneous translation for the delegates. My first Swiss friend was Mr Otto Wolfer from Freuzlingen. He spoke a little bit of Tibetan and had helped some Tibetan children in India.

The Tibet Institute in Rikon has been built up with the generous help of the Kuhn family, who manufacture metalware in Rikon, the Swiss aid for Tibetans and many private sponsors. Dr Lindegger, the first trustee of the Institute, worked very hard at the management and organization of the Institute.

On 28 September 1968 the Tibet Institute was inaugurated by the venerable Yongdsin Ling Rinpoche and the venerable Yongdsin Trijang Rinpoche, the two tutors of the Dalai Lama, and his representatives on this occasion. All geshes, lamas and Tibetans living in Europe attended the opening festivities. Finally, on 5 November 1968, the house was consecrated. Having moved into the house, I started teaching Dharma, meditation and Tibetan to Europeans.

In 1970 I went to Cambridge for three months, to improve my English. At that time I met a Buddhist group in Bromley, Kent, who invited me to give lectures every Saturday and Sunday and we also celebrated the Tibetan New Year together. I sometimes visited a nursery in the suburbs of London where there were a number of Tibetan children. Occasionally I went to London to visit a Thai monk.

Many Europeans are interested in the way Buddhism came to Tibet and to Sakya. I found that there are very few detailed books on the subject in the West so I thought it would be helpful to give all this basic information in one book. This is why the book *Historical acts on the Religion of the Sakya School* was written. Having finished it, I sent the text to the Sakya abbot in Darjeeling, who gave me some useful advice, and to His Holiness the Dalai Lama, asking for his consent. It is a very ancient tradition for a bodhisattva who has written a commentary on the Buddha's teachings to send the text to bodhisattvas and others to be checked. Then once I had received the consent of the community of monks of the Tibet Institute in Rikon, I published the book in 1970.

In 1973, we had the pleasure of welcoming His Holiness to the Tibet Institute in Rikon. Later in the year I went to India for five weeks. I went to Dharamsala, to see His Holiness the Dalai Lama, and then to Dehra Dun for a week, to see His Holiness Sakya Trizin. We were delighted to meet again, and had many conversations. I received many tantric teachings from His Holiness. I also visited our monastic community there, and offered a day's ceremony, called Lama Chöpa (*bla-ma-mchod-pa*). Then I visited my niece's son who was studying in the Tibetan high school in Sarnath, and took offerings to the monks of the great stupa there. From there I went to Bodhgaya, where I made offerings in front of the holy stupa and visited two spokesmen for His Holiness the Dalai Lama. Then I went to visit the Sakya monastery in Darjeeling where I had lived for two years, and made offerings to the monks there. My last visit was to my niece in South Mysore, where I stayed for a week, before returning to Switzerland.

In 1974 I worked for six months, together with Dr Stoll of the University of Zurich, on a Tibetan exhibition in the Museum of Ethnology. The exhibition was of religious statues and images, which Heinrich Harrer had brought from Tibet.

The same year, I invited His Holiness Sakya Trizin to come to Switzerland. He stayed for a month at the Institute, and gave teachings to the Tibetans. I also received some tantric teachings from him. His Holiness visited the universities of Zurich and Geneva and gave teachings at the Pestalozzi Children's Village in Trogen. In September 1974, His Holiness the Dalai Lama visited the Tibet Institute for a few days, and we were all very happy to see him again.

Since many Europeans came to the Institute wanting to learn the Tibetan language, I realized that there was no good Tibetan textbook for beginners. The only textbooks available for foreigners were those edited by the Council for Tibetan Education, which are mainly in classical Tibetan and very difficult for beginners. I thought it would be useful to write a book for those who did not know any Tibetan, as well as for Europeans and Tibetan foster-children who had come to the West a long time ago and now had difficulty in speaking Tibetan. I collected all the notes I had kept from my own Tibetan lessons and arranged them into the *Textbook for Colloquial Tibetan Language*. When it was finished, I sent it to the Council for Tibetan Education in Dharamsala for checking and the first edition of this book was published in 1974, the second in 1975.

In those days I was teaching religion and meditation to a group in Zurich. On 23 September 1974, I gave a lecture in the public hall in Zurich on the Buddhist tradition and the training of the mind. I also gave a one month course at the Tibet Institute on the Sakya school and the monastic tradition in Tibet.

Later that year, Michel and Sylviane Picard, an acupuncturist and his wife, came from Strasbourg to learn Buddhism and Tibetan. In February 1975 they invited me to Strasbourg to give a three day teaching on Buddhism and meditation. Since then, many people from Strasbourg have asked me to give teachings and from time to time I go there to teach.

In 1975 I was invited for the first time to Hanover, and gave teachings there for a week. I continued to teach there now and then the same year. Also that year I held a seminar on religion at the Tibet Institute for a month.

In 1976 an American monk whom I had taught returned to Switerland to continue his studies of religion and philosophy at the Institute. This monk had learnt Tibetan very well when he was in India, and he proposed to translate my book *Historical Acts on the Religion of the Sakya School* into English. This was completed under my supervision, under the title *A Waterdrop from the Glorious Sea*.

In 1976 I was invited to Holland to give teachings there for ten days. I visited the National Buddhist Society, the Theosophic Society and many Buddhist groups, yoga centres and youth organizations. I was particularly impressed with the Theosophic Society, where I gave a public lecture. The Theosophists, like the Buddhists, believe in karma and samsara. There was a little time left for me to do some sightseeing and I got the impression of a land completely surrounded by water. Meanwhile, the Dharma group in Den Haag, Sakya Thegchen Ling, was established, inviting me two or three times a year.

At the Tibet Institute in Rikon, my day begins with the prayers of the monk's community in the temple from seven to eight a.m. After breakfast I practise *The Four Profound Daily Meditations* and other sadhanas. For the rest of the day I teach religion and the Tibetan language, and I am also studying foreign languages myself. An American called Mark, who came to my lectures regularly for six months, taught me to type.

Every monk in the Institute, as part of the monastic community, has a particular job to do. It is my duty to show visitors around the Institute, to tell them about Dharma, and to explain the meaning of the different statues and thangkas. I find this very interesting as I get to know people from many different countries.

So until 1977 I continued in this way and made the acquaintance of a number of people who attended my teachings regularly. Among other subjects, they completed their studies in the *Bodhicaryavatara* and the *Nangsum-Sutra* of the Lam Dre. The enthusiasm and kindness of these diligent students were a source of much valuable inspiration.

In the course of that year, it was decided to found a Sakya

centre in Strasbourg. This centre, Sakya Tsechen Ling, was officially inaugurated on 13 February 1977. It has been growing ever since, and has become a European Buddhist Centre under my guidance. There were several reasons for the establishment of this centre in the small village of Kuttolsheim, near Strasbourg. Firstly because of the beautiful surroundings and the peaceful atmosphere of the Alsatian landscape, secondly because Kuttolsheim can be easily reached from all over Europe, with good transport facilities.

Of course it is a difficult task to found such a centre. The Europeans studying with us have to get accustomed to a new spiritual form and and to attain some understanding of the Buddhadharma, it will take time and they will have to practise patience to comprehend the essence of Buddhism. I am very grateful to all the friends and organizations who have helped us financially as well as to those who have so generously given their time in running the centre. Now I give monthly seminars on Buddhist philosophy and its practice in daily life.

In November 1977 I was invited to Freiburg in Germany by several people who had been studying Buddhadharma for some time. Since then I have been invited to go there four times a year, and in 1980 this group was named Yeshe Chöling. The members meet for meditation, study the Dharma and come to the teachings in Kuttolsheim.

Since 1978, I have been invited regularly to Lugano, where there is another group, called Thuptan Changchub Ling. The members meditate together and translate texts into Italian. These people, who come from the Italian Tessin and from Lugano, are very religious and try earnestly to understand the meaning of life and the essence of Dharma. In addition, I frequently give lessons to a group of Tibetans in Flawil in Switzerland.

In the summer of 1978 His Holiness Sakya Trizin accepted my invitation to come to the Tibet Institute in Rikon. During his month's stay, he gave many teachings and gave the Avalokitesvara intitiation to several hundred Tibetans. I was allowed to receive instructions and blessings from His Holiness myself, which filled me with great joy.

During his visit in September, His Holiness inaugurated the new house of the Sakya Tsechen Ling centre in Kuttolsheim, which has become the European Institute for Tibetan Buddhism. For this reason he gave teachings and initiations there, as well as in Strasbourg.

In 1979, I was invited to Hamburg for the first time by some people who practise Buddhist philosophy and meditation. In due course this small group was named Dechän Chöling, which means deep peace through the practice of Dharma. I go there occasionally to give teachings.

In 1980, the Dharma centre in Uppsala, Sweden was named Changchub Chöling. Sweden has impressed me by its great beauty and peace. I have a very harmonious relationship with the members of this group, because of their warmth and friendliness.

His Holiness Sakya Jigdal Dagchen Rinpoche, who lives in the United States at present, was invited by me to come to Switzerland for a month in 1980. From there he went to Kuttolsheim and to other centres to give precious teachings.

During this time, I was asked to republish my book, *Training of the Mind in Mahayana Buddhism*, in which I summarized the basic teachings as I explain them in some of my lectures. This proved to be very beneficial for those wishing to practise Buddhadharma.

On 19 October 1982 we had the honour to receive his Holiness the Dalai Lama at Sakya Tsechen Ling in Kuttolsheim. On the occasion of a public teaching in Strasbourg he explained the *Zenpa Zidel* (*The Parting from the Four Attachments*) to many Tibetans and Europeans. It was impressive to see people's interest in that subject. This was His Holiness's first visit to France, and he gave up some time to offer personal advice on the practice of the Dharma to some students. With gratitude and great delight, I participated in these and other important events, which are of inestimable value to so many people.

Later that year, the German translation of the *English Textbook of Colloquial Tibetan Language* was completed and in Spring 1984 the revised edition of my book *Training of the Mind in Mahayana Buddhism* was begun. The third edition is now available, and this is the English edition.

In summer and autumn 1984, together with some of the Dharma groups, I invited His Holiness Sakya Trizin for a third visit to Europe. We were so glad that His Holiness agreed to give the great Lam Dre teachings in Sakya Tsechen Ling. These precious, holy teachings originate from Mahasiddha Virupa and were passed down without interruption to the present Sakya Trizin, Ngawang Kunga.

'Lam Dre' means 'The path and its fruit.' It consists of a sutra part, the *Nangsum*, and of a tantric part, the *Gyud sum*, of which the Hevajra initiation, lasting two days, is the most important. It is very rare for these complete teachings to be given. It has only been done in India a few times, and now in Europe for the first time.

After His Holiness had taught in France, from August to September, he travelled for two months through five European countries, giving teachings and initiations. At the Tibet Institute in Rikon, which is within easy reach of Tibetans living in Switzerland, many people received teachings, initiations and blessings from His Holiness.

This is a short account of my life; and of the way Buddhism has spread in Europe, thanks to the growing interest of Western countries in Buddhadharma.

Glossary

Abhidharma   the section of the Buddhist canon dealing with metaphysics.

Arhat   one who has attained liberation from the suffering of cyclic existence.

Arya   a superior being, having attained direct realization of the true nature of reality.

Asura   a demi-god.

Atisha   (Dipankara-Shrijnyana) the great Indian pandit who came to Tibet around 1040 AD to help restore, purify and revive Tibetan Buddhism. Author or many works including the *Lamp for the Path* which condenses all Buddha's eighty-four thousand teachings into the lam rim – graduated path to enlightenment. He founded the school known as the Kadampa's from which the Gelug sect derives.

Avalokitesvara   the bodhisattva of all-encompassing compassion.

Bardo   the intermediary state between death and rebirth.

Bardo Thödol   a series of instructions originally composed by Padmasambhava explaining the mental projections experienced during the bardo process. Traditionally read to a dead or dying person, its transmission is powerful enough to awaken the mind of a well-trained practitioner to liberation, through hearing.

Bodhicitta   the enlightenment thought. There are two types of bodhicitta, relative and ultimate. The relative is also divided into two, wishing bodhicitta and entering bodhicitta. The first is the wish to liberate all sentient beings from the sufferings of samsara, the second the actual entry into the practice of the bodhisattva path. Ultimate bodhicitta is the ultimate truth which transcends all the mentally created extremes such as existence and non-existence, being and non-being, and so on, and is possessed by all Buddhas.

Bodhisattva   one who is entirely dedicated to the achievement of complete enlightenment. A bodhisattva takes the vow not to enter nirvana until the very last living creature has attained Buddhahood. Bodhisattvas therefore willingly re-enter the cycle of samsara with the aim of helping and supporting all living beings and leading them ultimately to the state of complete enlightenment.

Buddhadharma   the doctrine taught by Buddha leading to freedom from suffering and the ultimate goal of complete enlightenment.

Buddha   one who has attained full enlightenment, having abandoned all obscurations and accomplished all good qualities of wisdom, power and compassion.

Confessional Buddhas   each of the thirty-five Confessional Buddhas has the power to eliminate negative actions and obstacles of Dharma practice. Recitation of the *Sutra of the Three Heaps*, the confessional prayer to the thirty-five Buddhas, is an especially powerful method for purifying broken vows, and is usually performed along with prostrations.

Conqueror   epithet for a Buddha.

Dakini   emanation of a Buddha in female form.

Deva   a god.

Dharma   generally this applies to the doctrine comprising all the teachings of the Buddha, but it can also refer to the supreme law ruling over the genesis, the being and vanishing of all phenomena. In Tibetan texts phenomena in general are called dharma. Through meditational practice, Dharma is finally experienced as the ultimate truth.

Dharmadhatu   the ultimate sphere of reality, void and all-encompassing, in which phenomena arise, abide and pass away.

Dharmakaya the truth body of a Buddha, the omniscient mind of one who has attained full enlightenment.

Dharmapala a protector of the Dharma whose function is to guard the integrity of a practitioner's Dharma practice from both external and internal interferences.

Du-dha the principles of Buddhist logic.

Geshe a doctoral title conferred on those who have completed extensive studies and examinations at a monastic college.

Guru a spiritual guide; literally, one who is 'heavy' in spiritual attainment and therefore qualified to teach others.

Guru-yoga meditation and spiritual practices of guru devotion.

Hevajra a semi-wrathful male deity.

Hinayana of the three vehicles leading to liberation, the Hinayana is the path for the sravakas and pratyekabuddhas. It is called 'Hina-yana' or 'lesser vehicle' since unlike the Mahayana and Vajrayana paths it lacks the prerequisite strength of compassion needed to attain full enlightenment.

Jambu tree a wish-fulfilling tree whose fruit is enjoyed by the gods.

Kalpa a measurement of time used in Buddhist metaphysics equal to a long aeon.

Kanchen Bodhisattva (Shi-wa-tso, Sanskrit: Upadhyaya Santaraksita). Invited by King Trison Detson to Tibet he helped lay the foundations for Dharma in Tibet.

Kangyur the Tibetan translation of all the Buddha's teachings compiled into one hundred and eight volumes. This collection includes the *Vinaya* works (moral rules), the *Sutras* (teachings), the *Abhidharma* (metaphysics) and the *Tantras* (ritual and meditational instructions).

Karma the law of cause and effect. It is best expressed in the Buddha's own words:

Monks, I declare that karma is the result of premeditated deeds performed on purpose. They are the roots of either joy or sorrow. They cause rebirth in the round of existence (samsara).

Kaya   the body of a Buddha. There are four Buddha bodies: the nirmanakaya, sambhogakaya, jnanadharmakaya and svabhavikakaya (the last two can be included together as the dharmakaya).

Lama   see *Guru*.

Lam Dre   the path and its fruit; the principal teaching upheld by the Sakya sect.

Lokas   the six realms of existence: gods, demi-gods, humans, animals, pretas, hell-beings.

Lopon   the master in a monastery.

Madhyamika   philosophical school founded by the pandit Nagarjuna emphasizing the correct understanding of emptiness.

Mahakala   a wrathful deity who acts as protector of the Dharma; an emanation of Chenrezig. The first guru of the Mahakala lineage was an Indian by the name of Brahma Vararuci. When he was on his deathbed, he sent his protective deity to the holy place of Sakya, to Sachen Kunga Nyingpo. From that time on, Mahakala acted as the protector of the Sakya teachings.

Mahayana   the 'great vehicle,' the path of the bodhisattvas who motivated by great compassion strive to attain full enlightenment in order to place all sentient beings in that state. Also called the Paramitayana.

Maitreya   the next Buddha.

Mandala   form symbolizing the entire universe.

Manjushri   the bodhisattva of all-pervading wisdom.

Mantra   arrangement of sounds, syllables or phrases, usually Sanskrit, associated with various emanations of the Buddhas. Endowed with a special power they are generally recited in meditational practice.

Mo   a prophecy or means of divination.

Mount Sumeru   a huge mountain at the centre of each world system.

Nadis psychic channels through which the life supporting winds of the body flow.

Nirmanakaya the emanation body of a Buddha, the form in which a Buddha appears in the world.

Nirvana the ultimate goal of Dharma practice. For the Hinayanist this is liberation from samsara, for the Mahayanist it is the bliss of full enlightenment.

Padmasambhava (Guru Rinpoche) the great Indian saint who visited Tibet in the eighth century at the request of King Trison Detsun, spreading Buddha's teachings.

Pandita a very learned scholar. In general, one who has mastered the five main subjects of Indian science: the art of medicine, linguistics, Dharma and dialectics, as well as religious philosophy.

Paramita the six paramitas or perfections form the framework of a bodhisattva's spiritual practice. They are: giving, morality, patience, diligence, wisdom, meditation.

Pramana ideal cognition, being fresh, non-deceptive perception.

Pratimoksa individual liberation, especially referring to the monastic vows.

Pratyekabuddha one who attains liberation in one lifetime by following the Hinayana path but lacking the full realization of a Buddha is unable to lead others to that state.

Preta a hungry ghost.

Puja offering, usually refers to an act of worship.

Rabjampa degree conferred upon those who have successfully mastered the monastic study within the Sakya tradition.

Root Guru the principal guru from whom one has received teachings in this life.

Rupakaya the form bodies of a Buddha.

Sadhana a special meditational practice where the course of the meditation is laid down in detail.

Samadhi a highly advanced state of meditative concentration.

Samatha basic meditation practice used for calming the

mind in order to engage in vipassana (insight) meditation.

Samantabhadra a bodhisattva renowned for his generosity and extensive offerings.

Sambhogakaya the enjoyment body of a Buddha; the form in which a Buddha appears to arya bodhisattvas.

Samsara the continuous round of existence.

Sangha the absolute Sangha refers to the assembly of arya beings; the relative Sangha to those who have taken religious vows, especially monks and nuns.

Shakyamuni from the thousand Buddhas due to appear in this fortunate aeon, Guru Shakyamuni Buddha is the Buddha of this era.

Siddha one who possesses supernatural strength or ability attained through meditational practice.

Sravaka a follower of the Hinayana path who can attain liberation through hearing the teachings; lower than a pratyekabuddha.

Sukhavati the peaceful Buddhaland presided over by the Buddha Amitabha.

Sunyata the ultimate truth; the negation of the independent nature of all phenomena. Very often sunyata is misinterpreted as complete emptiness. It is not emptiness itself, however, but the non self-existent nature of the ego and all phenomena.

Sutra a teaching of the Buddha.

Svabhavikakaya the nature body of a Buddha; the void nature of a Buddha's omniscient mind.

Tangyur commentaries on the *Kangyur*, consisting of two hundred and twenty-five volumes written by Indian panditas.

Tantrayana see *Vajrayana*

Tara female embodiment of the compassion of all the Buddhas. She appears in many aspects but primarily white and green. Tibetans customarily recite prayers and praises to Tara in order to ensure success in whatever action they are undertaking.

Tathagata epithet for a Buddha, meaning 'One Gone Beyond' or 'Fully Perfected in all Qualities.'

Ten Non-virtuous Deeds these are divided into the three non-virtuous deeds of body: 1. killing, 2. stealing, 3. sexual misconduct; the four of speech: 4. lying, 5. ill repute, 6. bad speech, 7. empty talk; and the three of mind; 8. envy, 9. hatred, 10. wrong views.

Ten Virtuous Deeds the opposite of the ten non-virtuous deeds.

Three Impurities these are self-love, aversion to others, and ignorance of the true nature of all things.

Three Precious Jewels (the Three Gems) are the Buddha, Dharma and Sangha.

Tong-len the practice of giving and taking: giving one's own virtue and happiness to others and taking the suffering and non-virtue of others upon oneself. A supreme method for developing the mind of bodhicitta.

Tripitaka the 'Three Baskets' of the Buddha's teachings: the *Vinaya* (moral discipline), *Sutras* (discourses), *Abhidharma* (metaphysics).

Tulku the reincarnation of a previous enlightened being.

Vajra a tantric ritual implement symbolizing indestructibility.

Vajradhara the aspect in which Buddha taught the *Tantras*.

Vajrapani the bodhisattva embodying the power of all the Buddhas.

Vajrasattva an aspect of the Buddha's enlightened mind associated with purification, the recitation of whose mantra is particularly effective in purifying negative karmas from the mind's continuum.

Vajrayana the swiftest of the three vehicles to enlightenment. It offers the means by which a faithful disciple can attain Buddhahood within a single lifespan provided he has the help of a qualified teacher and his mind has reached a suitable level of spiritual maturity.

Vajra Yogini   a semi-wrathful female deity.

Vipassana   insight meditation, penetrating into the nature of reality.

Yana   a vehicle or path leading to liberation and enlightenment. The three yanas are Hinayana, Mahayana and Tantrayana.

Yidam   the main deity around which a tantric practitioner focuses his practice.

Yoga   physical and mental techniques for developing and purifying the mind.

Yogin/Yogini   a male/female practitioner of yoga.

Suggested Further Reading

From the Sakya tradition

Amipa, Geshe Sherab Gyaltsen, *A Waterdrop from the Glorious Sea*, Rikon, Tibetan Institute, 1979.

Nagarjuna and Sakya Pandita, *Elegant Sayings*, Berkeley, Dharma Publications, 1977.

Trichen Rinpoche, Chogay, *The History of the Sakya Tradition*, Bristol, Ganesha Press, 1983.

General

Atisha, *A Lamp for the Path and Commentary*, Richard Sherburne (tr.), London, George Allen & Unwin, 1983 (Wisdom of Tibet Series, 5).

Gyatso, Tenzin, the Fourteenth Dalai Lama, *The Buddhism of Tibet* and *The Key to the Middle Way*. London, George Allen and Unwin, 1975.

———, *Kindness, Clarity and Insight*, New York, Gabriel Snow Lion, 1984.

———, *Opening the Eye of New Awareness*, London, Wisdom Publications, 1985.

Rabten, Geshe and Dhargyey, Geshe Ngawang, *Advice from a Spiritual Friend*. London, Wisdom Publications, 1976; 1986.

Shantideva, *A Guide to the Bodhisattva's Way of Life*, Batchelor, Stephen (tr.), Dharamsala, Library of Tibetan Works and Archives, 1979; 1985.

Rabten, Geshe, *The Preliminary Practices of Tibetan Buddhism*, Dharamsala, Library of Tibetan Works and Archives, 1976; 1982.

Yeshe, Lama Thubten and Zopa Rinpoche, *Wisdom Energy*, London, Wisdom Publications, 1982; 1984.

Publisher's Acknowledgement

The publisher would like to thank an anonymous donor from Taiping, Malaysia, for her kind sponsorship of this book.

She herself wishes that her merit be dedicated to the long life of His Holiness Sakya Trizin and all other teachers showing the paths to happiness, liberation and enlightenment.